Ernest Renan

English Conferences of Ernest Renan

Rome and Christianity. Marcus Aurelius

Ernest Renan

English Conferences of Ernest Renan
Rome and Christianity. Marcus Aurelius

ISBN/EAN: 9783744778695

Printed in Europe, USA, Canada, Australia, Japan

Cover: Foto ©ninafisch / pixelio.de

More available books at **www.hansebooks.com**

ENGLISH CONFERENCES

OF

ERNEST RENAN.

ROME AND CHRISTIANITY.
MARCUS AURELIUS.

TRANSLATED BY

CLARA ERSKINE CLEMENT.

BOSTON:
JAMES R. OSGOOD AND COMPANY.
1880.

COPYRIGHT, 1880,
BY JAMES R. OSGOOD & COMPANY.

Franklin Press:
Stereotyped and Printed by
Rand, Avery, & Co.,
Boston.

CONTENTS.

	PAGE.

THE HIBBERT CONFERENCES.

First Conference. The Sense in which Christianity is a Roman Work 9

Second Conference. The Legend of the Roman Church. — Peter and Paul 39

Third Conference. Rome, the Centre of the Formation of Ecclesiastical Authority 73

Fourth Conference. Rome, the Capital of Catholicism 103

THE ROYAL INSTITUTION CONFERENCE.

Marcus Aurelius 139

NOTE.

THE lectures contained in this volume were delivered by M. ERNEST RENAN in London during April of the present year. The first four, upon "Rome and Christianity," were given under the auspices of "The Hibbert Foundation," in response to an invitation under which the distinguished author visited England. The fifth, "Marcus Aurelius," was incidental to the visit, and was given before "The Royal Institution." The word "Conferences," though somewhat new to English usage in its present sense, has been retained as best expressing the author's original title, "*Conferences d'Angleterre.*"

ROME AND CHRISTIANITY.

FIRST CONFERENCE,

London, April 6, 1880.

THE SENSE IN WHICH CHRISTIANITY IS A ROMAN WORK.

FIRST CONFERENCE.

THE SENSE IN WHICH CHRISTIANITY IS A ROMAN WORK.

Ladies and Gentlemen, — I was proud and happy to receive from the curators of this noble institution an invitation to continue here an instruction inaugurated by my illustrious confrère and friend, Max Müller, the usefulness of which will be more and more appreciated. A broad and sincere thought always bears fruit. It is thirty years since the venerable Robert Hibbert made a legacy for the purpose of aiding the progress of enlightened Christianity, inseparable, according to his idea, from the progress of science and reason. Wisely carried out, this foundation has become, in the hands of intelligent administrators, the centre of conferences upon all the great chapters of the history of religion and humanity: the promoters of this reform have asked, with reason, why the method which has proved good in all departments of intellectual culture should not also be good in the domain of religion? why the pursuit of truth, without regard to consequences, should be dangerous in theology, when it is approved of in the entire domain of social and natural science? You believed the truth, gentlemen, and you were right. There is but one truth; and we are wanting in respect to its revelation, if we allow that the critic ought to soften his severe processes when he treats of it. No, gentlemen, the truth is able to dispense with compliments. I come gladly at your call; for I understand the duties towards the right exactly as you do. With you, I should believe that I injured a faith in admitting that it required to be treated with a certain softness. I believe with you that the worship due from man to the ideal consists in independent scientific research, without regard to results, and that the true manner of rendering homage to the truth is to pursue it without ceasing, with the firm resolution of sacrificing all to it. You desire that these conferences shall present a great historic *ensemble* of the efforts which the human race has made to resolve the problems which surround it, and affect its destiny. In the present state of the human mind, no one can hope to resolve these problems: we suspect all dogmatism simply because it is dogmatism. We grant willingly that a religious or philosophical system can, indeed, or that it ought to, enclose a certain portion of truth; but we deny to it, without examination, the possibility of enclosing the absolute truth. What we love is history. History well written is always good; for, even if it should prove that man in seeking to seize the infinite has pursued a chimera, the history of these attempts, more generous than successful, will always be useful. It proves, that, in reality, man goes beyond the circle of his limited life through his aspirations. It shows what energy he has expended for the sake of his love of the good and true; it teaches us to estimate him,— this poor disinherited one, who, in addition to the sufferings which nature imposes upon him, imposes still further upon himself the torture of the unknown, the torture of doubt, the severe resistances of virtue, the abstinences of austerity, the voluntary sufferings of the ascetic. Is all this a pure loss? Is this unceasing effort to attain the unattainable as vain as the course of the child who pursues the ever flying object of his desire? It pains me to believe it; and the faith which eludes me when I examine in detail each of the systems scattered throughout the world, I find, in a measure, when I reflect upon all these systems together. All religions may be defective and incomplete; religion in humanity is nothing less than divine, and a mark of superior destiny. No, they have not labored in vain — those grand founders, those reformers, those prophets of all ages — who have protested against the false evidences of gross materialism, who have beaten themselves against the wall of the apparent fatality that encloses us; who have employed their thought, given their life, for the accomplishment of a mission which the spirit of their age had imposed upon them. If the fact of the existence of the martyrs does not prove the exclusive truth of this or that sect (all sects can show a rich martyrology), this fact in general proves that religious zeal responds to something mysterious. All, — as many as we are, — we are sons of martyrs. Those who talk the most of scepticism are frequently the most satisfied and indifferent. Those who have founded among you religious and political liberty, those who have founded in all Europe liberty of thought and research, those who have labored for the amelioration of the fate of men, those who will doubtless find means for further amelioration, have suffered, or will suffer, for their good work; for no one is ever recompensed for what he does for the good of humanity. Nevertheless they will always have imitators. There will always be some to carry on the work of the incorrigibles; some, possessed of the divine spirit, who will sacrifice their personal interest to truth and justice. Be it so: they have chosen the better part. I know not what assures me that he who, without knowing why, through simple nobility of nature, has chosen for himself in this world the essentially unproductive lot of doing good, is the true sage, and has discovered the legitimate use of life with more sagacity than the selfish man.

I.

You have asked me to retrace before you one of those pages of religious history which places the thoughts which I come to express in their fullest aspect. The origins of Christianity form the most heroic episode in the history of humanity. Man never drew from his heart more devotion, more love of the ideal, than in the one hundred and fifty years which elapsed from the sweet Galilean vision, under Tiberius, to the death of Marcus Aurelius. The religious consciousness was never more eminently creative, and never laid down with more authority the law of the future. This extraordinary movement, to which no other can be compared, came forth from the bosom of Judaism. But it is doubtful if Judaism alone would have conquered the world. It was necessary that a young and bold school, coming out of its midst, should take the audacious part of renouncing the largest portion of the Mosaic ritual. It was necessary, above all, that the new movement should be transported into the midst of the Greeks and Latins, while awaiting the Barbarians, and become like yeast in the bosom of those European races by which humanity accomplishes its destinies. What a beautiful subject he will discourse upon who shall one day explain to you the part which Greece took in that great common work! You have commissioned me to show to you the part of Rome. The action of Rome is the first in date. It was scarcely until the beginning of the third century that the Greek genius, with Clement of Alexandria and Origen, really seized upon Christianity. I hope to show you, that, since the second century, Rome has exercised a decisive influence upon the Church of Jesus.

In one sense, Rome has diffused religion through the world, as she has diffused civilization, as she has founded the idea of a central government, extending itself over a considerable part of the world. But even as the civilization which Rome has diffused has not been the small, narrow, austere culture of ancient Latium, but in fact the grand and large civilization which Greece created, so the religion to which she definitely lent her support was not the niggardly superstition which was sufficient to the rude and primitive inhabitants of the Palatine: it was Judaism, that is to say, in fact, the religion which Rome scorned and hated most, that which two or three times she believed herself to have finally vanquished to the profit of her own national worship. This ancient religion of Latium, which contented a race endowed with narrow intellectual wants and morals, among which customs and social rank almost held the place of a religion during some centuries, was a sufficiently despicable thing. As M. Boissier has perfectly proved, a more false conception of the divinity was never seen. In the Roman worship, as in most of the ancient Italiote worships, prayer was a magic formula, acting by its own virtue, independent of the moral dispositions of him who prayed. People prayed only for a selfish end. There exist some registers called *indigitamenta*, containing lists of the gods who supply all the wants of men; thus there was no need of being deceived. If the god was not addressed by his true name, by that under which it pleased him to be invoked, he was capable of misapprehension, or of interpreting capriciously. Now these gods, who are in some degree the forces of the world, are innumerable. There was a little god who made the infant utter his first cry (*Vaticanus*); there was another who presided over his first word (*Fabulinus*); another who taught the baby to eat (*Educa*); another who taught him to drink (*Potina*); another who made him keep quiet in his cradle (*Cuba*). In truth, the good wife of Petronius was right, when, in speaking of the Campagna, she said, "This country is so peopled with divinities, that it is easier to find a god than a man." Besides these, there were unending series of allegories, or deified abstractions, Fear, the

Cough, Fever, Manly Fortune, Patrician Chastity, Plebeian Chastity, the Security of the Age, the Genius of the Customs (or of the *octroi*), and above all (listen, that one who, to say the truth, was the great god of Rome), the Safety of the Roman People. It was a civil religion in the full force of the term. It was essentially the religion of the State. There was no priesthood distinct from the functions of the State: the State was the veritable god of Rome. The father had there the right of life and death over his son; but if this son had the least function, and the father met him in his path, he descended from his horse, and bent himself before him.

The consequence of this essentially political character was, that the Roman religion remained always an aristocratic religion. A man became pontiff as he became prætor or consul. When a man desired these religious functions, he submitted to no examination; he went into no retreat in a seminary; he did not ask himself whether he had the ecclesiastical vocation: he proved that he had served his country well, and that he had been wounded in a certain battle. There was no sacerdotal spirit. These civil pontiffs remained cold, practical men, and had not the least idea that their functions should separate them from the world. The religion of Rome is, in every respect, the inversion of theocracy. Civil law rules acts:

it does not trouble itself with thoughts; thus did the Roman religion. Rome never had the least idea of dogma. The exact observation of the rites commanded by the divinity, in which it did not regard piety or the sentiments of the heart, if the request was in form, was all that was required. Even more, — devotion was a fault; calmness, order, regularity, only, were necessary: more than that was an excess (*superstitio*). Cato absolutely forbade that a slave should be allowed to conceive any sentiment of piety. "Know," said he, "that it is the master who sacrifices for all the household." It was not needful to neglect what was due to the gods; but it was not needful to give them more than was due: that was superstition, of which the true Roman had as much horror as of impiety.

Was there ever, I ask you, a religion less capable of becoming the religion of the human race than that? Not only was the access to the priesthood for a long time forbidden to the plebeians, but they were also excluded from the public worship. In the great struggle for civil equality which fills the history of Rome, religion is the great argument with which the revolutionists are opposed. "How," say they, "could you become a prætor or consul? You have not the right to take the omens." Above all, the people were very little attached to religion. Each popular victory was followed, as one may say, by an anti-clerical re-action: on the contrary, the aristocracy remained always faithful to a worship which gave a divine sanction to its privileges.

The matter became still more pressing when the Roman people, by their manly, patriotic virtues, had conquered all the nations upon the borders of the Mediterranean. What interest, think you an African, a Gaul, a Syrian, took in a worship which concerned only a small number of high and often tyrannical families? The local religions were continued everywhere; but Augustus, who was still more a religious organizer than a great politician, made the Roman idea to hover everywhere by the establishment of the Roman worship. The altars of Rome and of Augustus became the centre of a hierarchical organization of Flamens and Augustan *Sevirs*, who served to found, more than one imagines, the divisions of the dioceses and ecclesiastical provinces. Augustus admitted all the local gods as Lares; he allowed more than the number of Lares in each house; at each cross-road an additional Larẹ was placed, — the Genius of the Emperor. Thanks to this fellowship, all the local gods and all the special gods became " Augustan gods." It was a great advance. But this grand attempt of the worship of the Roman State was notoriously insufficient to satisfy the religious needs of the heart. There was elsewhere a god who could not accommodate himself in any way to this fraternity: it was the God of the Jews. It was impossible to make Jehovah pass for a Lare. and associate with the Genius of the Emperor. It was evident that a conflict must be established between the Roman State and this unchangeable and refractory God, who did not bend to the complaisant transformations exacted by the politics of the times.

Ah, well! behold the most extraordinary historical phenomenon, the most intense irony of all history: it is that the worship which Rome has diffused through the world is not in the least the old worship of Jupiter Capitolinus, or Latiaris, still less the worship of Augustus and of the Genius of the Emperor: it is, in truth, the worship of Jehovah. It is Judaism in its Christian form that Rome has propagated, without wishing it, in so powerful a manner, that, from a certain epoch, Romanism and Christianity have become almost synonymous words.

Truly, I repeat it, it is more than doubtful if pure Judaism — that which is developed under the Talmudical form, and which is still in our day so powerful — would have had this extraordinary fortune. Judaism propagates itself through Christianity. But one understands nothing of religious history (some one, I hope, will demonstrate it to you some day), unless it is fixed as a fundamental principle that Christianity had its origin in Judaism itself, — Judaism with its fruitful principles of alms and charity, with its absolute confidence in the future of humanity, with that joy of the heart of which it has always had the secret, — only Judaism freed from some observances and distinctive traits which had been invented to characterize the special religion of the children of Israel.

II.

IF one studies in fact the progress of the primitive Christian missions, he remarks that they are all directed towards the West: in other words, they take the Roman Empire as their theatre and limit. If one excepts some small portions of the vassal territory of the Arsacidæ, lying between the Euphrates and the Tigris, the empire of the Parthians received no Christian missions during the first century. The Tigris was an eastern boundary which Christianity did not pass under the Sassanidæ. Two great causes — the Mediterranean and the Roman Empire — determined this capital fact.

The Mediterranean had been, during a thousand years, the great route on which all civilizations and all ideas had passed each other. The Romans, having freed it from piracy, had made it an unequalled way of communication. It was in a sense the railroad of that time. A numerous marine of coasting-vessels rendered the voyages along the borders of this great lake very easy. The relative security which the routes of the empire afforded, the sure guaranties found in the public powers, the scattering of the Jews over all the coasts of the Mediterranean, the use of the Greek tongue in the eastern portion of this sea, the unity of civilization which the Greeks first, and then the Romans, had created, made the map of the empire also the map of the countries reserved to the Christian missions and destined to become Christian. The Roman *orbis* became the Christian *orbis* in the sense in which it may be said that the founders of the empire were the founders of the Christian monarchy, or, at least, that they have drawn its outlines. Every province conquered by the Roman Empire became a province conquered by Christianity. Let the figures of the apostles be imagined in the presence of Asia Minor, of Greece, of Italy divided into a hundred little republics, of Gaul, of Spain, of Africa, of Egypt, with its old national institutions, and their success can no more be thought of, or rather it would seem that their project could never have had birth. The union of the empire was the necessary preliminary condition of all great religious propagandism, placing it above nationalities. The empire recognized this in the fourth century. It became Christian. It saw that Christianity was the religion which it had accepted without knowing it, — the religion limited by its frontiers, identified with it, capable of bringing it a second life.

The Church, on its side, made itself entirely Roman, and has remained to this day a fragment of the empire. During the middle ages the Church was the old Rome, seizing again its authority over the barbarians, imposing on them its decretals, as formerly it had imposed its laws, governing them by its cardinals, as it had before governed through its imperial legates and proconsuls.

In creating its vast empire, Rome imposed, then, the material condition of the propagation of Christianity. She raised up, above all, the moral state which served as an atmosphere and a medium for the new doctrine. While destroying politics everywhere, it created what may be called socialism and religion. At the close of the frightful wars which for some centuries had rent the world, the empire had an era of prosperity and of welfare such as it had never known: we may even be permitted to add (without a paradox) liberty. Liberty of thought, at least, increased under this new *régime*. This liberty is often more prosperous under a king or a prince than under the jealous and narrow-minded plebeian. The ancient republics did not have it. The Greeks did great things without it, thanks to the incomparable power of their genius; but it must not be forgotten that Athens had a fine and noble Inquisition. The king Archon was the inquisitor; the royal Portico was the holy office in which the accusations of impiety were adjudged. These were the cases in which the Attic orators were most frequently engaged. Not only philosophical crimes, such as the denial of God or of a Providence, but the lightest attaint of the municipal worship, the preaching of strange religions, the most puerile infractions of the scrupulous legislation of the mysteries, were crimes guilty of death. The gods whom Aristophanes mocked on the stage sometimes destroyed. They destroyed Socrates; they failed to kill Alcibiades. Anaxagoras, Protagoras, Diagoras of Melas, Prodicus of Ceos, Stilpo, Aristotle, Theophrastus, Aspasia, Euripides, were more or less seriously disturbed. Liberty of thought was, in truth, the fruit of the royalties resulting from the Macedonian conquest. It was the Attali, the Ptolemies, who first gave to men of thought the freedom which no one of the old republics had ever offered them. The Roman Empire held to the same traditions. There was under the empire more than one arbitrary law against the philosophers; but these always resulted from their meddling with political affairs. In the laws of the Romans, before the time of Constantine, no clause is found against the liberty of thought; in the history of the emperors, no process of abstract doctrine. No *savant* was disturbed in his researches. Men whom the middle ages would have burned, such as Galen, Lucian, Plotinus, lived tranquilly, protected by law. The empire inaugurated a period of liberty in the sense that it destroyed the absolute sovereignty of the family, the city, the tribe, and replaced or modified these sovereignties by those of the State. Now, an absolute power is as much more vexatious as the circle in which it is exercised is more narrow. The ancient republics, the feudalities, tyrannized over the individual much more than did the State. Unquestionably the Roman Empire persecuted Christianity severely at times; but at least it did not destroy it. Now the republics would have rendered it impossible. Judaism, if it had not been under the Roman authority, would have stifled it. It was the Roman magistrates who hindered the Pharisees from killing Christianity. Some lofty ideas of universal brotherhood — results, in the main, of stoicism, — a sort of general sentiment of humanity, were the fruit of the least narrow *régime* and of the least exclusive education to which the individual was submitted. The people dreamed of a new era and new worlds. The public riches were great; and, in spite of the imperfection of the economical doctrines of the time, there was general comfort.

General customs were not such as are often imagined. It is true, that, in Rome, all the vices were publicly displayed with a revolting cynicism: the spectacles, above all, had introduced a frightful corruption. Certain countries, as Egypt, had descended to the lowest baseness. But there existed in most of the provinces a middle class, in which goodness, conjugal fidelity, the domestic virtues, and uprightness were commonly practised. Does there anywhere exist, in a world of honest people in small villages, an ideal of family life more charming than that which Plutarch has left us? What good fellowship! What sweetness of manners! What chaste and attractive simplicity! Chæronea was evidently not the only place where life was so pure and so innocent.

The customs, even outside of Rome, were still somewhat cruel, either through the remaining spirit of ancient manners, everywhere sanguinary, or through the special influence of Roman harshness. But there was progress during this period. What sweet and pure sentiment, what feeling of melancholy tenderness, has not found expression by the pen of Virgil or of Tibullus? The world unbent, lost its ancient severity, and acquired some softness and tenderness. Some maxims for humanity were spread abroad. Equality and the abstract idea of the rights of man were boldly preached by stoicism. Woman became more and more the mistress of herself. The precepts for the treatment of slaves were improved. The slave was no longer that necessarily grotesque and wicked being which the Latin comedy introduced in order to provoke bursts of laughter, and whom Cato recommended to be treated as a beast of burden. Now, times are much changed. The slave is morally equal to his master: it is admitted that he is capable of virtue, of fidelity, of devotion, and he gives proofs of it. The prejudices concerning noble birth grow less. Some very humane and just laws are made, even under the worst emperors. Tiberius was a skilful financier: he founded upon an excellent basis an establishment of *crédit foncier*. Nero inaugurated in the system of taxation, until then unjust and barbarous, some improvements which shame even our own time. Legislation was considerably advanced, while the punishment of death was stupidly prodigal. Love of the poor, sympathy for all, and almsgiving, came to be considered virtues.

III.

UNQUESTIONABLY I understand and share the indignation of sincere liberals against a government which diffused a frightful despotism over the world. But is it our fault that the wants of humanity are diverse, its aspirations manifold, its aims contradictory? Politics is not every thing here below. What the world desired, after those frightful butcheries of the earlier centuries, was gentleness, humanity. They had enough of heroism: those vigorous goddesses, eternally brandishing their spears on the height of the Acropolis, inspired sentiment no longer. The earth, as in the time of Cadmus, had swallowed her most noble sons. The proud Grecian races had killed each other. The Peloponessus was a desert. The sweet voice of Virgil gently took up the cry of humanity, peace, pity!

The establishment of Christianity responded to this cry of all tender and weary souls. Christianity could only have had birth and expansion in a time when there were no longer free cities. If there was any thing totally lacking in the founders of the Church, it was patriotism. They were not cosmopolites, for the entire planet was to them a place of exile: they were idealists in the most absolute sense.

A country is a composition of soul and body. The soul is the souvenirs, the legends, the customs, the misfortunes, the hopes, the common sorrows: the body is the soil, the race, the language, the mountains, the rivers, the characteristic productions. Now, was a people ever more wanting in all this than the first Christians? They did not cling to Judæa; after a few years they had forgotten Galilee; the glory of Greece and Rome was indifferent to them. The countries in which Christianity was first established — Syria, Cyprus, and Asia Minor — no longer remembered the time when they were free. Greece and Rome, it is true, still had a grand national sentiment. At Rome, patriotism survived in a few families; in Greece, Christianity flourished only at Corinth, — a city which, since its destruction by Mummius, and its reconstruction by Cæsar, was the resort of men of all races. The true Greek countries, then, as to-day, very jealous, very much absorbed in the memories of their past, gave little countenance to the new doctrines: they were always lukewarm Christians. On the contrary, those gay, indolent, voluptuous countries of Asia and Syria, countries of pleasure, of free manners, *de laisser aller*, accustomed to receive life and government from others, had nothing to resign in the way of pride and traditions. The most ancient capitals of Christianity — Antioch, Ephesus, Thessalonica, Corinth, and Rome — were common cities, so to speak, cities of the modern type of Alexandria, in which all races met, where that marriage between man and the soil, which constitutes a nation, was absolutely broken.

The importance given to social questions is always the inverse of political pre-occupations. Socialism takes the lead when patriotism grows weak. Christianity exploded the social and religious ideas, as was inevitable, since Augustus had put an end to political struggles. Christianity, if a universal worship, would, like Islamism, in reality be the enemy of nationalities. Only centuries, only schisms, could form national churches from a religion which was from the beginning a denial of all terrestrial countries, which had its birth at an epoch in which there were no longer in the world either cities or citizens, and which the old and powerful republics of Italy and of Greece would surely have expelled as a mortal poison to the State.

And here was one of the causes of the grandeur of the new religion. Humanity is a multiform, changeable thing, tormented by conflicting desires. *La patrie* is grand, and the heroes of Marathon and Thermopylæ are saints. But one's country is not all here below: one is a man and a son of God, before he is a Frenchman, or a German. The kingdom of God, an eternal dream which is never destroyed in the heart of man, is a protestation against a too exclusive patriotism. The thought of an organization of humanity, in view of its greatest happiness and its moral amelioration, is legitimate. The State knows, and can only know, one thing, — to organize a collective egoism. This is not indifference, because egoism is the most powerful and seizable of human motives, but is not sufficient. The governments which have rested upon the supposition that man is composed of covetous instincts only, have deceived themselves. Devotion is as natural as egoism to a true-born man. The organization of devotion is religion: let no one hope, then, to dispense with religion, or religious associations. Each progression of modern society will render this want more imperious.

A great exaltation of religious sentiment was, then, the consequence of the *Roman peace* established by Augustus. Augustus realized it. But I ask, What satisfaction could the institutions which Rome dared to believe eternal present to the religious wants which were arising? Surely almost nothing. All the old worships, of very different origin, had one common trait. They shared equally the impossibility of reaching a theological teaching, a practical morality, an edifying preaching, a pastoral ministry truly fruitful for the people. The Pagan temple, in its best time, was the same thing as the synagogue and the church: I wish to say the common house, the school, the inn, the hospital, the shelter in which the poor sought an asylum, it was a cold *cella*, into which one seldom entered, where one learned nothing. The affectation which led the Roman patricians to distinguish the "religion," that is to say, their own worship, from the "superstition," that is to say, the worship of strangers, appears to us puerile. All the Pagan worships were essentially superstitious. The peasant who in our day places a sou in the box of a miraculous chapel, who invokes some saint on account of his oxen, or his horses, who drinks certain waters for certain maladies, is in these acts a Pagan. Indeed, nearly all our superstitions are the remains of a religion anterior to Christianity, which that has not been able to entirely uproot. If one would find the image of Paganism in our day, it must be sought in some obscure village in the depth of some out-of-the-way country.

Having as guardians a popular, vacillating tradition, and selfish sacristans, the Pagan religion could but degenerate in worship. Augustus, although, with a certain reserve, accepted the adoration of his subjects in the provinces. Tiberius allowed, under his own eyes, that ignoble concourse of the cities of Asia to dispute the honor of raising a temple to him. The extravagant impieties of Caligula produced no re-action: outside of Judaism there was not found a single priest to resist such follies. Coming forth, for the most part, from a primitive worship of natural forces ten times transformed by minglings of all sorts, and by the imagination of the peoples, the Pagan worships were limited by their past. One could never draw from them what had never existed in them, — Deism or instruction. The fathers of the church amuse us when they bring to notice the misdeeds of Saturn as the father of a family, and of Jupiter as a husband. But without doubt it was still more ridiculous to set up Jupiter (that is to say, the atmosphere) as a moral god who commands, defends, rewards, and punishes. In a world which aspires to possess a catechism, what could one do with a worship like that of Venus, which arose from an old social necessity of the first Phœnician navigation in the Mediterranean, but became in time an outrage to that which one regards more and more as the essence of religion?

Here is the explanation of that singular attraction, which, towards the commencement of our era, drew the populations of the Old World towards the worships of the East. These worships had something more profound than the Greek and Latin worships: they appealed, moreover, to the religious sentiment. Almost all were relative to the state of the soul in another life, and they were believed to contain some pledges of immortality. From this arose that favor which the Thracian and Sabasian mysteries enjoyed, the worshippers of Bacchus, and brotherhoods of all sorts. There was less of coldness in these little circles, in which one pressed against another, than in the great glacial world elsewhere. Some minor religions, like that of Pysche, destined solely to console for death, had immense popularity. Those noble Egyptian worships which concealed the emptiness within by grand splendor of ceremonies counted their devotees throughout the empire. Isis and Serapis had their altars at the extremities of the world. In visiting the ruins of Pompeii, one would be tempted to believe that the worship of Isis was the principal one practised there. Those little Egyptian temples had some assiduous devotees, among whom were counted a large number of persons of the class of the friends of Catullus and Tibullus. There was a service each morning, — a sort of mass, celebrated by a tonsured and beardless priest; there were some sprinklings of holy water, and perhaps an evening service: it occupied, amused, and quieted. What more is necessary?

But, more than all others, the Mithraic worship enjoyed in the second and third centuries an extraordinary popularity. I sometimes allow myself to say, that, had not Christianity taken the lead, Mithraicism would have become the religion of the world. Mithraicism had mysterious reunions, and chapels which strongly resembled little churches. It established a very solid bond of brotherhood between its votaries; it had the Eucharist, the Lord's Supper, and bore such a resemblance to the Christian mysteries, that the good Justin the Apologist saw only one explanation of these resemblances: it is that Satan, in order to deceive the human race, sought to mimic the Christian ceremonies, and committed this plagiarism. The Mithraic tomb of the Catacombs of Rome is as edifying and deeply mysterious as the Christian tombs. There were some devoted Mithraists, who, even after the triumph of Christianity, defended the sincerity of their faith with courage. The people grouped themselves around these foreign gods: around the Greek and Italiote gods there were no gatherings. We must say a good word for it: it is only the small sects that lay the foundation and build up. It is so sweet to believe one's self a little aristocracy of truth, to imagine, that, in common with a very few, one owns the repository of truth! Such a foolish sect in our own time gives to its adherents more consolation than a more healthy philosophy. In his day, Abracadabra secured some joyous followers, and, by means of a little good-will, a sublime theology has been found in him.

We shall see, however, in our next conference, that the religious reign of the future belonged neither to Serapis, nor to Mithra. The predestined religion grew imperceptibly in Judæa. This would have greatly astonished the most sagacious Romans, if had been announced to them. It would have been shocking to them in the highest degree. But so often in history have improbable predictions become true, so often has wisdom been mistaken, that it is not best to rely too much upon the likes and dislikes of enlightened men, of *bons esprits* as we say, when they undertake to predict the future.

SECOND CONFERENCE,

London, April 9, 1880.

THE LEGEND OF THE ROMAN CHURCH. — PETER AND PAUL.

SECOND CONFERENCE.

PETER AND PAUL.

Ladies and Gentlemen, — At our last meeting we attempted to show the situation of the Roman Empire in regard to religious questions during the first century. There was in the vast gathering of populations which composed the empire a pressing want of religion, a true moral progress, which called for a pure worship without superstitious practices or bloody sacrifices; a tendency to Monotheism, which made the old mythological recitals appear ridiculous; a general sentiment of sympathy and of charity, which inspired the desire of association, of assembling together for prayer, for support, for consolation, for the assurance that after death one would be interred by his brethren, who would also make a little feast in his memory. Asia Minor, Greece, Syria, and Egypt contained masses of the poor, — very honest men, after their manner, humble, and without distinction; but revolted at the spectacle which the Roman aristocracy made, full of horror at those hideous representations in the theatres, in which Rome made a diversion of suffering. The moral conscience of the human race sent up an immense protestation, and there was no priest to interpret it, no pitying God to reply to the sighs of poor suffering humanity. Slavery, in spite of the protestations of the sages, remained very cruel. Claudius thought to do a grand and humane act in making a law that the master who should drive from his house an old and sick slave should lose his right in that slave, if he were cured. How could gods without compassion, and born of joy and the primitive imagination, be expected to console for such evils? A Father in heaven was required, who kept a record of the efforts of man, and promised him a recompense. A future of justice was desired, in which the earth belonged to the feeble and the poor. The assurance was necessary, that, when a man suffered, it was not an entire loss, and that beyond those sad horizons, veiled by tears, there were happy fields in which one day he should console himself for his sorrows. Judaism indeed had all that. By the institution of the synagogues (do not forget, gentlemen, that it is from the synagogue that the church comes), it established association in the most powerful form in which it had ever been realized. In appearance, at least, the worship was pure Deism; no images, only scorn and sarcasm for idols. But that which above all characterized the Jew was his confidence in a brilliant and happy future for humanity. Having no idea based upon the immortality of the soul, nor upon the remunerations and punishments beyond the tomb, the Jew, disciple of the ancient prophet, was as if intoxicated with the sentiment of justice: he wished justice now upon earth. Having little confidence in the assurances of the eternity which made the Christians so easily resigned, the Jew grumbled at Jehovah, reproached him with his ignorance, and demanded how he could leave the earth so long in the power of the impious. As for himself, he did not doubt that the earth would one day be his, and that his law would make love and justice to reign therein.

In this struggle, gentlemen, the Jew will be victorious. Hope, that which the Jew calls the *Tiqva*, that assurance of something which nothing proves, but to which one attaches himself with so much the more frenzy because it is not sure, is the soul of the Jew. His psalms were like the continuous sound of a harp, filling life with harmony and a melancholy faith: his prophets held the words of eternity. For example, that second Isaiah, the prophet of the captivity, pictured the future with more dazzling colors than man had ever seen in his dreams. The Thora, besides that, gives the recipe for being happy (for being happy here below, I mean), by observing the moral law, the spirit of the family, and the spirit of duty.

I.

The establishment of the Jews at Rome dated nearly sixty years before Jesus Christ. They multiplied rapidly. Cicero represented it as an act of courage to dare to oppose them. Cæsar favored them, and found them faithful. The people detested them, thought them malevolent, accused them of forming a secret society whose members were advanced at any price, to the detriment of others. But all did not approve these superficial judgments. The Jews had as many friends as detractors: something superior was noticeable in them. The poor Jewish colporter of the Trastevere often in the evening returned home rich with the charities received from a pious hand. Women, above all, were attracted by these missionaries in rags. Juvenal counts the weakness towards the Jewish religion among the vices of the ladies of his time. The word of Zachariah was verified to the letter: the world seized upon the garments of the Jews, and said, " Lead us to Jerusalem."

The principal Jewish quarter of Rome was situated beyond the Tiber, that is to say, in the poorest and dirtiest part of the city, probably near the present *Porta Portese*. There, or rather opposite to the foot of the Aventine, the gate of Rome was formerly situated, where the merchandise brought from Ostia in barges was discharged. It was a quarter of Jews and Syrians, — "nations born for servitude," as Cicero said. The nucleus of the Jewish population at Rome was formed, in truth, of freedmen, descended, for the most part, from those prisoners whom Pompey had carried there. They had passed through slavery, without changing their religious customs in the least. That which is admirable in Judaism is that simplicity of faith which makes the Jew, transported a thousand leagues from his country, at the end of several generations, always a very Jew. The intercourse between the synagogues of Rome and Jerusalem was continual. The first colony had been re-enforced with numerous emigrants. These poor men disembarked by hundreds at the Ripa, and lived together in the adjacent quarter of the Trastevere, serving as street-porters, engaged in small affairs, exchanging matches for broken glasses, and showing to the proud Italiote populations a type which later became too familiar to them, — that of the beggar accomplished in his art. A Roman who respected himself never placed his foot in these abject quarters. It was as a suburb given up to despised classes and to infectious employments: the tanneries, the gut-works, the rotting vats were banished there. These unhappy people lived tranquilly enough in this remote corner, in the midst of bales of merchandise, low inns, and porters of manure (*Syri*), who had there their general headquarters. The police only entered there when affrays were bloody, or occurred too often. Few quarters of Rome were so free: politics had nothing to do there. Worship was not only practised there in ordinary times without obstacles, but its propagation was also accomplished with great facility.

Protected by the disdain which they inspired, caring little, moreover, for the railleries of the men of the world, the Jews of the Trastevere led a very active religious and social life. They had some schools of *hakamin:* nowhere was the ritual and ceremonial of the law observed more scrupulously: the organization of the synagogue was the most complete ever known. The titles of "father and mother" of the synagogues were much prized. Some rich converts took biblical names; they brought their slaves into the church with them, they had the Scriptures explained by the doctors, built places of prayer, and manifested their pride of the consideration which they enjoyed in this little world. The poor Jew found the means, while begging with a trembling voice, to whisper in the ear of the great Roman lady some words of the law, and frequently won over the matron who opened to him her hand full of small coin. To observe the sabbath and the Jewish feasts was to Horace the trait which classed a man in the crowd of weak minds. The universal benevolence, the happiness of reposing with the just, the assistance of the poor, the purity of manners, the gentle acceptance of death considered as a sleep, are some of the sentiments which are found in the Jewish inscriptions, with that particular accent of touching unction, of certain hope, which characterizes the Christian inscriptions. There have been many rich and powerful Jews in the world, such as Tiberius Alexander, who arrived at the greatest honors of the empire, who exercised two or three times the strongest influence upon public affairs, and even had, to the great grief of the Romans, his statue in the Forum; but those were not good Jews. The Herods, though practising their worship at Rome with much show, were also far from being true Israelites, even if their only sins were their relations with the Pagans.

A world of ideas was thus set in motion on the vulgar quay where the merchandise of the whole world was piled up; but all that would be lost in a great city like Paris. Undoubtedly the proud patricians, who, in their promenades on the Aventine, cast their eyes upon the other side of the Tiber, did not imagine the future that was forming itself in that little cluster of poor houses at the foot of Janiculum.

Near the port was a sort of lodging-house well

known to the people and the soldiers under the name of *Taberna Meritoria.* In order to attract the loungers, a pretended spring of oil coming out of a rock was shown there. From a very early time this spring of oil was considered by the Christians as symbolic: it was pretended that its appearance was coincident with the birth of Jesus. It seems that later the *Taberna* became a church. Under Alexander Severus we find the Christians and the inn-keepers in a contest over a place which formerly had been public: that good emperor gave it to the Christians. This is probably the origin of the Church of the Santa Maria of the Trastevere.

It is natural that the capital should have fully accepted the name of Jesus before the intermediate countries could be evangelized, as a high summit is lighted up while the valleys between it and the sun are still obscure. Rome was the rendezvous for all the Oriental worships, — the point upon the coast of the Mediterranean with which the Syrians had the most intercourse. They arrived there in enormous bands. Like all the poor populations rising for the assault of the great cities to which they come to seek their fortunes, they were serviceable and humble. All the world spoke Greek. The ancient Roman plebeians, attached to the old customs, lost ground each day, drowned as they were in this wave of strangers.

We admit then, that towards the year 50 of our era, some Syrian Jews, already Christians, entered the capital of the empire, and communicated the faith which rendered them happy to their companions. At this time no one suspected that the founder of a second empire was in Rome, — a second Romulus, lodging at the port in a bed of straw. A little band was formed. These ancestors of the Roman prelates were poor, dirty, common people, without distinction, without manners, clothed with fetid garments, having the bad breath of men who are badly fed. Their dwellings had that odor of misery which is exhaled from persons grossly clothed and nourished, and huddled together in narrow rooms. We know the names of two Jews who were the most prominent in these movements. They were Aquila, a Jew, originally from Pontus, who was like St. Paul an upholsterer, and Priscilla his wife, — a pious couple. Banished from Rome they took refuge at Corinth, where they soon became the intimate friends of St. Paul, and zealous workers with him. Thus Aquila and Priscilla are the most ancient known members of the Church of Rome. There is scarcely a souvenir of them there. Tradition, always unjust, because it is always ruled by political motives, has expelled these two obscure workmen from the Christian Pantheon in order to attribute the honor of the foundation of the Church of Rome to a name more in keeping with its proud pretensions. We do not see the original point of the origin of Occidental Christianity in the theatrical Basilica consecrated to St. Peter: it is at that ancient *Ghetto*, the *Porta Portese*. It is in tracing these poor vagabond Jews, who bore with them the religion of the world, — these suffering men, dreaming in their misery of the kingdom of God, — that we shall find it again. We do not dispute with Rome its essential title. Rome was probably the first point in the Western World, and even in Europe, where Christianity was established.

But, instead of these lofty basilicas, in place of these insulting devices, — *Christus vincit, Christus regnat, Christus imperat*, — it would be better to raise a poor chapel to these good Jews who first pronounced on the quay of Rome the name of Jesus.

A capital trait, which it is important to note in any case, is, that the Church of Rome was not, like the churches of Asia Minor, Macedonia, and Greece, a foundation of the school of Paul. It was fundamentally Judæan-Christian, re-attaching itself directly to the Church of Jerusalem. Paul here will never be on his own ground: he will find in this great church many weaknesses which he will treat with indulgence, but which will wound his exalted idealism. Attached to circumcision and outward observances, Ebionite through its taste for abstinences, and by its doctrine concerning the person and death of Jesus more Jewish than Christian, leaning strongly towards Millenarianism, the Roman Church showed, since its first days, the essential traits which will distinguish it through its long history. Own daughter of Jerusalem, the Roman Church will always have an ascetic, sacerdotal character, opposed to the Protestant tendencies of Paul. Peter will be its veritable head; then, the political and hierarchical spirit of old Rome penetrating it, it will indeed become the new Jerusalem, the city of the Pontificate, of the hieratic and solemn religion, of the material sacraments which justify of themselves, the city of the ascetics of the manner of Jacques Ohliam with his callous knees and his plate of gold upon his brow. It will be the authoritative church. If we can believe it, the only mark of the apostolic mission will be to show a letter signed by the apostles, to produce a certificate of orthodoxy. The good and the evil which the Church of Jerusalem did in giving birth to Christianity, the Church of Rome will do for the Universal Church. It is in vain that Paul will address to it his beautiful epistle to explain the mystery of the cross of Jesus and of salvation by faith alone. The Church of Rome will scarcely comprehend it; but Luther four and a half centuries later will comprehend it, and will open a new era in a secular series of the alternate triumphs of Peter and Paul.

II.

An important event in the history of the world took place in the year 61. Paul was led a prisoner to Rome in order to follow up the appeal which he had made to the tribunal of the emperor. A sort of profound instinct had always made Paul desire this journey. His arrival at Rome was almost as marked an event in his life as his conversion. He believed that he had attained the summit of his apostolic life; and doubtless he recalled the dream in which, after one of his days of struggle, Christ had appeared to him, and said, "Be of good cheer, Paul; for as thou hast testified of me in Jerusalem, so must thou bear witness also at Rome."

You will not forget the wide divisions which separated the disciples of Jesus during the first century from the foundation of Christianity,— divisions so broad, that all the differences which to-day separate the orthodox, the heretics, and the schismatics of the whole world, are nothing beside the dissensions of Peter and Paul. The Church of Jerusalem, obstinately attached to Judaism, refused all intercourse with the uncircumcised, however pious they might be. Paul, on the contrary, thought that to maintain the ancient law was an injury to Jesus, since thus it might be supposed, that, outside the merits of Jesus, such or such a work could serve for the justification of the faithful. However strange it may appear, it is certain that the Judæan-Christians of Jerusalem, with James at their head, organized some active contra-missions in order to combat the effect of the missions of Paul, and that the emissaries of these ardent conservatives followed in some sort the lead of the apostle of the Gentiles. Peter belonged to the party at Jerusalem, but showed in his conduct that sort of timid moderation which seems to have been the foundation of his character. Did Peter also come to Rome? Formerly, gentlemen, this question was one of the most exciting which could be agitated. Formerly the history of religion was written, not to recount it, but in order to prove it: religious history was an annex of theology. During the grand revolt, so full of courage and of ardent conviction, which, during the sixteenth century, placed one-half of Europe in opposition to Rome, the negation of the sojourn of Peter at Rome became a sort of dogma. The Bishop of Rome is the successor of St. Peter, said the Catholics, and as such the head of Christendom. How could that reasoning be more strongly refuted than by maintaining that Peter never placed his foot in Rome?

As for us, we are permitted to regard this question with the most perfect disinterestedness. We do not believe, in any sense, that Jesus intended to give any head whatever to his church; and above all, it is doubtful whether the idea of such a church as developed later had existed in the mind of the founder of Christianity. The word *ecclesia* occurs only in the Gospel of St. Matthew. The idea of the *episcopos*, as it existed in the second century, had no place in the mind of Jesus. He himself was the living *episcopos* during his brief Galilean appearance: from that time it is the Spirit who inspires each one until he may return. In any case, if it had been possible that Jesus should have had any idea whatever of the *ecclesia* and *episcopos*, it is absolutely beyond doubt, that Jesus never thought of giving the future *episcopos* of the city of Rome to be the head of his church, — that impious city, the centre of all the impurities of the earth, of whose existence he perhaps knew scarcely any thing, and of which he should have entertained the gloomy opinions which all the Jews professed. If there is any thing in the world which was not instituted by Jesus, it is the Papacy, that is to say, the idea that the Church is a monarchy. We are, then, perfectly at liberty to discuss the question of Peter's coming to Rome. This question is absolutely without consequence for us; and from our solution the only result will be to say whether Leo XIII. is or is not the head of the Christian conscience. Whether Peter was or was not in Rome, it has for us no political nor moral bearing. It is a curious question of history: it is useless to pursue it further.

First, let us say, that the Catholics have laid themselves open to the peremptory objections of their adversaries by their unfortunate reckoning of the coming of Peter to Rome in the year 42, — a reckoning borrowed from Eusebius and St. Jerome, which extends the duration of the pontificate of Peter to twenty-three or twenty-four years. There is nothing more inadmissible. In order to leave no doubt in regard to this, it is sufficient to consider that the persecution of Peter at Jerusalem by Herod Agrippa occurred in the year 44. It would be superfluous to oppose longer a thesis which can have no one reasonable defence. It is possible, in fact, to go much further, and to affirm that Peter had not yet come to Rome when Paul was taken there, that is to say, in the year 61. The Epistle of Paul to the Romans, written about the year 58, is a very considerable argument here. One can scarcely imagine St. Paul writing to the faithful, of whom St. Peter was the head, without making the least mention of the latter. The last chapter of the Acts of the Apostles is still more demonstrative. This chapter, especially from the seventeenth to the twenty-ninth verse, cannot be explained, if Peter was at Rome when Paul arrived there. Let us, then, consider it absolutely certain that Peter did not come to Rome before Paul, that is to say, before or about the year 61.

But did he not come there after Paul? This has never been positively proved; this late journey of Peter's to Rome was not only probable, but there are strong arguments in its favor. Besides the testimony of the Fathers of the second and third centuries, there are three reasons which do not appear to me unworthy : —

1st, It is indisputably certain that Peter suffered a martyr's death. The testimony of the fourth evangelist, of Clement Romanus, of the fragment which is called the "*Canon de Muratori*," of Denis of Corinth, of Caius, of Tertullian, leave no doubt in this respect. Let the fourth Gospel be apochryphal, allow that chapter xxi. has been added in later times, it makes no difference. It is clear, that, in the verses in which Jesus announces to Peter that he shall die by the same suffering as his own, we have the expression of an opinion established in the Church about 120 or 130, to which allusions are made as to a fact known to all. Now, it is not possible to imagine that Peter died a martyr outside of Rome. It was only at Rome, in fact, that the persecution of Nero was violent. At Jerusalem, at Antioch, the martyrdom of Peter would have been much less probable.

2d, The second reason is found in the Epistle attributed to St. Peter (v. 13): "The church that is at Babylon . . . saluteth you." Babylon, in this passage, evidently indicates Rome. If the Epistle is authentic, the passage is decisive: if it is apocryphal, the conclusion to be drawn from the text is not weakened. The author, in short, whoever he may be, wishes it to be regarded as the work of Peter. He was consequently forced, in order to give an appearance of truth to his fraud, to arrange the circumstances which he related, according to what he knew, or believed was known in his time, of the life of Peter. If, in such a spirit, he dated the letter at Rome, it shows, that, in his day, it was the general opinion that Peter had resided at Rome. But, in any case, the First Epistle of Peter is a very ancient work, and had very early a high authority.

3d, The theory which is founded upon the Ebionite Acts of St. Peter is also worthy of much consideration. This theory represents St. Peter as following Simon the Magician everywhere (according to St. Paul), in order to dispute his false doctrines. M. Lipsius has shown an admirable critical sagacity in his analysis of this legend. He has shown that the base of all the different versions of it which have come to us was written about the year 130. It seems improbable that an Ebionite author of such early date could have given so much importance to Peter's journey to Rome, if this journey had not taken place in reality. The theory of the Ebionite legend must contain some truth at the bottom, in spite of the fables which are mingled with it. It is quite admissible that St. Peter might have come to Rome, as he went to Antioch, following St. Paul, and in part to neutralize his influence. The missions of St. Paul, and the facility which the Jews had acquired in their voyages had made long expeditions quite the custom. The apostle Philip is even represented by an ancient and persistent tradition as having settled himself in Hierapolis, in Asia Minor.

I regard, then, as probable, the tradition of the sojourn of Peter at Rome; but I believe that this sojourn was short, and that Peter suffered martyrdom soon after his arrival in the Eternal City.

III.

You know the mystery which hovers above the history of primitive Christianity, which we might desire to know more in detail. The death of the apostles Peter and Paul remains enveloped in a veil which will never be penetrated. That which appears the most probable is, that they both disappeared in the great massacre of Christians commanded by Nero.

On the 19th of July, in the year 64, a violent fire burst out at Rome. It originated in that portion of the great Circus near to the Palatine and Cœlian Hills. In this quarter there were many little shops, filled with inflammable matter, in which the flames spread with prodigious rapidity. Thence it made the turn of the Palatine, ravaged the Velabra, the Forum, the Carinæ, ascended the hills, greatly injured the Palatine, descended again to the valleys, devouring compact quarters, and piercing tortuous streets, continuing six days and seven nights. An enormous pile of houses which were torn down near the foot of the Esquiline, arrested its progress for a time; then it again broke out, and endured three days more. A considerable number of people perished. Of the fourteen portions which composed the city, three were entirely destroyed; of seven, only blackened walls remained. Rome was an extremely compact city, and the population very dense. This disaster was frightful, and the like of it had never before been seen.

When the fire broke out, Nero was at Antium. He returned to the city about the time when it approached his "transitory" house. It was not possible to arrest the flames. The imperial houses of the Palatine, the "transitory" house itself with its dependencies, and the whole surrounding quarter, were destroyed. Nero did not seem much to regret the loss of his house. The sublime horror of the spectacle transported him. Later it was said that he had watched the fire from a tower, where, in a theatrical costume, with a lyre in his hand, he chanted the ruin of Ilion to the rhythm of an ancient elegy.

This was a legend, the fruit of a period of successive exaggerations; but one point upon which the universal opinion was decisive from the first was, that Nero had commanded this fire, or at least had revived it when it seemed about to die out.

These suspicions were confirmed by the fact, that, after the fire, Nero, under pretext of removing the ruins at his own cost, in order to leave the place free to the proprietors, undertook to clear away the *débris;* and the people were not allowed to approach. This seemed worse when it was seen that he drew from the ruins what belonged to the country, when the new palace, that "golden house" which had been the plaything of his delirious imagination, was seen rising upon the site of the ancient provisory residence, enlarged by the spaces which the fire had cleared.

It was believed that he had desired to prepare the place for his new palace, to justify the reconstruction which he had long contemplated, to procure money by appropriating the wreck of the fire, in short, to satisfy his mad vanity, which led him to desire to rebuild the whole of Rome, so that it might date from him, and be called Neropolis.

All the honest men of the city were outraged. The most precious antiquities of Rome, the houses of the ancient leaders, decorated with triumphal spoils, the most holy objects, the trophies, the ancient *ex-votos*, the most revered temples, all the belongings of the old worship of the Romans, had disappeared. It was as if they mourned the souvenirs and the traditions of the whole country. They celebrated expiatory services; they consulted the books of the Sibyl: the ladies especially observed various *piacula*. But the secret consciousness of a crime and infamy still remained.

Then an infernal idea took possession of the mind of Nero. He cast about to see if he could find anywhere some miserable wretches, still more detested by the Roman plebeians than himself, upon whom he could rest the odium of the incendiarism. He thought of the Christians. The horror which they testified towards the temples and the most venerated edifices of the Romans made the idea plausible, that they should have been the authors of this fire, the result of which was the destruction of these sanctuaries. Their air of sadness in regarding the monuments appeared like an injury to the nation. Rome was a very religious city, and whoever protested against the national worship was at once remarked. It should be remembered that certain rigorous Jews went so far as to refuse to touch money which bore an effigy: they even saw a great crime in bearing or looking at an image, unless engaged in the occupation of carving. Others refused to pass beneath a city gate surmounted by a statue. All this excited the ridicule and ill-will of the people. Perhaps the idea that the Christians were incendiaries gained force from their manner of talking about the final conflagration, their sinister prophecies, their love of reiterating that the world would soon be ended, and ended by fire. It is even admissible that some of the faithful might have committed imprudences, and that there were pretexts for accusing them of having wished, by anticipating the celestial flames, to justify their oracles, at any price. Four and a half years later the Apocalypse was to present a chant upon the burning of Rome, for which the event of 64 probably furnished more than one feature. The destruction of Rome by fire had been a Christian and Jewish dream; and it was not merely a dream: the pious sectaries were pleased to see in spirit the saints and angels applauding from the heights of heaven what they regarded as a just expiation.

A certain number of persons suspected of belonging to the new sect were arrested, and thrown into prison, which was of itself a punishment. The first arrests were followed by many others. The people were surprised at the multitude of converts who had accepted these gloomy doctrines: it was only spoken of with alarm. All sensible men considered the accusation of having caused the fire as extremely weak. "Their true crime," said they, "is hatred of the human race." Although persuaded that the burning was the crime of Nero, many serious Romans saw in this work of the police a mode of delivering the city from a dreadful nuisance. Tacitus, in spite of his pity, was of this opinion. And Suetonius counted the sufferings which Nero heaped upon the partisans of the new and mischievous superstitions as among his laudable measures.

These sufferings were something frightful. Such refinements of cruelty had never been seen. Almost all those arrested were of the *humiliores* (the poorest classes). The sentence of these unfortunates, when it concerned high treason or sacrilege, was to be thrown to the beasts, or to be burned alive in the amphitheatre. One of the most hideous traits of Roman manners was that of making a *fête*, a public amusement, of these tortures. The amphitheatres had become places of execution: the tribunals furnished the victims. The condemned of the entire world were forwarded to Rome for the provisioning of the circus and the amusement of the people. At this time derision was added to the barbarism of these tortures. The victims were kept for a feast day, to which was given, without doubt, an expiatory character. "The morning spectacle," consecrated to the combats of animals, presented an appearance hitherto unknown. The condemned, covered with the tawny skins of beasts, were hurried into the arena, where they were torn by dogs. Some were crucified: others, reclothed with tunics steeped in oil, wax, or resin, were bound to posts, and reserved to light up the evening *fêtes*. When the day lowered, these living torches were ignited. For this spectacle, Nero offered his magnificent gardens beyond the Tiber, which occupied the site of the present Borgo, the Square, and the Church of St. Peter. Near by was a circus commenced by Caligula, in which the middle of the *Spina* was marked by an obelisk brought from Heliopolis (the same one which in our day stands in the centre of the Square of St. Peter). This place had already been the scene of massacres by the light of torches. Caligula, in one of his walks, decapitated a certain number of consular personages, senators, and Roman ladies, by the light of torches. The idea of replacing lanterns by human bodies impregnated with inflammable substances had occurred to the ingenious Nero. Burning alive was not a new mode of suffering; it was the ordinary penance of incendiaries: but it had never been made a system of illumination. By the light of these hideous torches, Nero, who had established the custom of evening entertainments, showed himself in the arena, sometimes mingling with the people in the dress of a charioteer, sometimes conducting his chariot and seeking applause. Women and young girls were involved in these horrible games: a *fête* was made of the nameless indignities which they suffered. Under Nero, the custom was established of compelling the condemned to play in the amphitheatre some mythological part entailing the death of the actor. These hideous operas, where mechanical science attained to prodigious effects, were very popular. The miserable wretch was introduced into the arena, richly costumed as god or hero devoted to death. He then represented by his suffering some tragic scene of the fables consecrated by sculptors and poets. Sometimes it was the furious Hercules burned on Mount Œta, tearing the waxed tunic from his skin; sometimes Orpheus torn in pieces by a bear; Dædalus thrown from heaven, and devoured by beasts; Pasiphæ struggling in the embraces of the bull; Attys murdered. Sometimes there were horrible masquerades, in which the men were dressed like priests of Saturn with a red cloak, the women as priestesses of Ceres with fillets on the brow· finally, at other times, some dramatic work of the time, in which the hero was really condemned to death as Laureolus; or the representations were those of such tragic acts as that of Mucius Scævola. At the end of these hideous spectacles, Mercury, with a red-hot iron wand, touched each corpse to see if it moved. Some masked valets, dressed like Pluto or Orcus, dragged away the dead by the feet, killing with hammers all who still breathed. The Christian ladies of the highest respectability even suffered these monstrosities. Some played the *rôle* of the Danaïdes, others that of Dirce. It is difficult to say what fable furnishes a more bloody picture than that of the Danaïdes. The suffering which all mythological tradition attributes to these guilty women was not cruel enough to suffice for the pleasure of Nero and the *habitués* of his amphitheatre. Sometimes they were led out bearing urns, and received the fatal blow from an actor figuring as Lynceus. Sometimes these unhappy beings went through the series of the sufferings of Tartarus before the spectators, and only died after hours of torments. The representations of Hell were quite *à la mode*. Some years previous (the year 41), some Egyptians and Nubians came to Rome, and made a great success in giving evening performances, in which they displayed in order the horrors of the subterranean world, conforming to the paintings of the burial-places of Thebes, notably those of the tomb of Seti I.

As for the sufferings of the Dirces, there was no doubt about them. People know the colossal group now in the Museum of Naples, called the *Toro Farnese*, — Amphion and Zethus attaching Dirce to the horns of an unmanageable bull, which is to drag her over the rocks and briers of Cithæron. This mediocre Rhodian marble, brought to Rome in the time of Augustus, was the object of universal admiration. How could there be a finer subject for the hideous art which the cruelty of the time had made in vogue, and which consisted in reproducing the celebrated statues in living tableaux? An inscription and a fresco of Pompeii seem to prove that this terrible scene was frequently repeated in the arenas, when a woman was the sufferer. Naked, attached by the hair to the horns of a furious bull, these poor wretches glutted the eyes of a ferocious people. Some of the Christians immolated in this way were feeble in body: their courage was superhuman. But the infamous crowd had eyes alone for their torn bowels and lacerated bosoms.

After the day when Jesus expired in Golgotha, the *fête* day in the Gardens of Nero (it may be fixed about the first of August, 64) was the most solemn in the history of Christianity. The solidity of any construction is in proportion to the sum of virtue, of sacrifices, and of devotion which has been laid down at its base. Only fanatics lay foundations. Judaism endures still on account of the intense frenzy of its zealots; Christianity, on account of its first witnesses. The orgy of Nero was the grand baptism of blood which set Rome apart as the city of martyrs in order to play a distinct *rôle* in the history of Christianity and to be the second Holy City. It was the taking possession of the Vatican Hill by conquerors hitherto unknown there. The odious, hair-brained man who governed the world did not perceive that he was the founder of a new order, and that he signed a charter for the future, the effects of which would be claimed after eighteen hundred years.

IV.

As we have said, it is allowable, without improbability, to connect the deaths of the apostles Peter and Paul with the account which we have just given. The only historical incident known, by which the martyrdom of Peter can be explained, is the episode recounted by Tacitus. Some solid reasons also lead us to believe that Paul suffered the death of a martyr at Rome. It is then natural to suppose that he also died in the massacre of July and August, 64. As to the manner of death of the two apostles, we know with certainty that Peter was crucified. According to some ancient writings, his wife was executed with him, and he saw her led to the sacrifice. One accepted account of the third century says, that, too humble to equal Jesus, he suffered with his head down. The characteristic trait of the butchery of 64 having been the search for odious rarities in torture, it is possible that in truth Peter was shown to the crowd in this hideous attitude. Seneca mentions some cases in which tyrants have been known to turn the heads of the crucified towards the earth. Christian piety has seen a mystical refinement in that which was indeed an odd caprice of the executioner. Perhaps this extract from the Fourth Gospel — "Thou shalt stretch forth thy hands, and another shall gird thee, and carry thee whither thou wouldest not" — includes some allusion to a peculiarity in the suffering of Peter. Paul, in his quality of *honestior*, had his head cut off. It is also probable that he was judged regularly, and that he was not included in the summary condemnations of the victims in the *fête* of Nero. All that, I repeat, is doubtful, and of little importance. True or not, the legend is believed. At the commencement of the third century, near Rome, there were already seen two monuments bearing the names of Peter and Paul. One was situated at the foot of the Vatican Hill, that of St. Peter: the other, in the way to Ostia, was that of St. Paul. They were called in oratorial style the trophies of the apostles. In the fourth century two basilicas were raised above these trophies. One of them is the present basilica of St. Peter: the other, St. Paul-without-the-Walls, has retained its essential features until our own century.

Did the trophies which the Christians venerated about the year 200 designate the spots upon which these apostles suffered? It is possible. It is not unlikely that Paul, toward the end of his life, dwelt in the suburb which extended beyond the Lavernal gate as far as the pine of the Salvian springs in the way to Ostia. The shade of Peter, on the other hand, wanders always, according to the Christian legend, towards the turpentine-tree of the Vatican, not far from the gardens of the Circus of Nero, and especially about the obelisk. It may be that the ancient place of the obelisk in the sacristy of St. Peter, now indicated by an inscription, is nearer to the place where St. Peter upon the cross of his frightful agony surfeited the eyes of a populace greedy to see him suffer. However, that is a secondary question. If the basilica of the Vatican does not really cover the tomb of St. Peter, it points out not the less for our remembrance one of the spots most truly hallowed by Christianity. The place which the seventeenth century surrounded with a theatrical colonnade was a second Calvary; and, even supposing that Peter was not crucified there, at least we cannot doubt the sufferings of the Danaïdes and the Dirces.

We shall show in our next assembly how tradition disposes of all these doubts, and how the Church consummates reconciliation between Peter and Paul, which death perhaps began. This was the price of success. The Judæan-Christianity of Peter and the Hellenism of Paul, apparently irreconcilable, were equally necessary to the success of the future work. The Judæan-Christianity represented the conservative spirit without which nothing is solid; Hellenism, advance and progress, without which nothing truly exists. Life is the result of a conflict between two contrary forces. The absence of all revolutionary spirit is as fatal as the excess of revolution.

THIRD CONFERENCE,

London, April 13, 1880.

ROME,

THE CENTRE OF THE FORMATION OF ECCLESIASTICAL AUTHORITY.

THIRD CONFERENCE.

ROME THE CENTRE OF THE FORMATION OF ECCLESIASTICAL AUTHORITY.

I.

Almost always the nations created to play a part in universal civilization, like Judæa, Greece, and the Italy of the renaissance, exercise their full action upon the world, only after becoming victims to their own grandeur. They must first die; then the world lives on them, assimilates to itself that which they have created at the price of their fever and their sufferings. Nations ought to choose in fact between the long, tranquil, obscure destiny of that which lives for itself, and the troubled, stormy career of that which lives for humanity. The nation which works out social and religious problems in its own bosom is almost always weak politically. Every country which dreams of a kingdom of God, which lives for general ideas, which pursues a work of universal interest, sacrifices through the same its individual destiny, enfeebles and destroys its *rôle* as a terrestrial country. One can never set himself on fire with impunity. Since Judæa made the religious conquest of the world, it was necessary that she should disappear as a nation. A revolution of extreme violence broke out in this country in the year 66. During four years, this strange race, which seemed created to defy equally that which blessed and that which cursed it, was in a convulsion before which the historian should pause with respect as he would before all mystery.

The causes of this crisis were very old, and the crisis itself was inevitable. The Mosaic law, a work of exalted Utopians possessed of a powerful socialist ideal, — the least politic of men, — was, like the Islam, exclusive of a civil society parallel with a religious society. This law, which appears to have been drawn up, as we now read it, in the seventh century before Jesus Christ, would have been the means of destroying the little kingdom of the descendants of David, even without the Assyrian conquest. Since the preponderance assumed by the prophetic element, the kingdom of Judah — embroiled with all its neighbors, seized with a permanent rage against Tyre, hating Edom, Moab, and Ammon — could no longer survive. I repeat, a nation which devotes itself to social and religious problems neglects its politics. The day in which Israel became "a peculiar people of God, a kingdom of priests, a holy nation," it was written that she should no longer be a nation as other nations. Contrary destinies cannot be united: an exaltation is always expiated by an abasement.

The Achemenidean kingdom gave Israel little repose. This grand feudality, tolerant towards all provincial differences, almost analogous to the Califat of Bagdad and to the Ottoman Empire, was the rule under which the Jews found themselves most at ease. The Ptolemaic rule in the third century before Jesus Christ seemed equally sympathetic to them: there were even no Seleucidæ. Antioch had become an active centre of Hellenic propagandism. Antiochus Epiphanus felt it necessary to set up everywhere the image of Jupiter Olympus as the sign of his power. Then broke out the first great Jewish revolt against profane civilization. Israel had patiently supported the disappearance of its political existence since Nebuchadnezzar. It retained no measure in which it saw a danger to its religious institutions. A race, in general not military, was seized with an access of heroism; without a regular army, without generals, without tactics, it conquered the Seleucidæ, maintained its revealed rights, and created a second period of autonomy. The Asmonean royalty, nevertheless, was always distracted by profound interior vices. It endured but one century. The destiny of the Jewish people was not to constitute a separate nationality. That people dreamed always of something international. Its ideal was not the city, it was the synagogue, the free congregation. The same is true of the Islam, which has created an immense empire, but has destroyed all nationality, in the sense in which we understand it, among the peoples which it has subjugated, and leaves them no other country than the mosque and the *Zaouia*.

The name of theocracy is often applied to such a social condition, and rightly so, if we mean by it that the profound idea of the Semitic religions, and of the empires which came out from them, is the kingdom of God considered as the master of the world, and universal suzerain. But theocracy with these nations was not synonymous with the domination of priests. The priest, properly speaking, plays an unimportant *rôle* in the history of Judaism and Islamism. The power belongs to the representative of God, — to him whom God inspires, to the prophet, to the holy man, to him who has received his mission from Heaven, and who proves his mission by a miracle, that is to say, by success. In default of a prophet, the power belongs to the author of apocalypses, and of apocryphal books attributed to the ancient prophets, or, better, to the doctor who interprets the divine law, to the head of the synagogue, and, still more, to the head of the family who guards the depository of the law, and transmits it to his children. A civil power, a royalty, has little to do with such social organization. This organization never works better than among spread-out peoples, under the rights of tolerated foreigners, in a grand empire where uniformity does not rule. It is the nature of Judaism to be politically subordinate, since it cannot draw from its own bosom a principle of military power. Its *animus* has been to form communities with their own laws and their own magistrates in the midst of other states, until modern liberalism introduced the principle of the equality of all before the law.

The Roman rule, established in Judæa sixty-three years before Christ by the armies of Pompey, seemed at first to realize some of the conditions of Jewish life. Rome at this epoch did not pursue the policy of assimilating the countries which she annexed to her vast empire. She robbed them of the right of peace and war, and arrogated to herself only the arbitration in great political questions.

Under the degenerated remains of the Asmonean dynasty and under the Herods, the Jewish nation preserved a half independence, in which its religious state was respected. But the interior feeling of the people was too strong. Beyond a certain degree of religious fanaticism, man is ungovernable. It should be said that Rome strove without ceasing to render her power in the East more effective. The little vassal kingdoms which she had at first preserved, disappeared day by day, and the provinces made returns to the empire pure and simple. The administrative customs of the Romans, even in their most reasonable aspects, were odious to the Jews. In general, the Romans showed the greatest condescension to the fastidious scruples of the nation; but that was not sufficient: things had come to a point where nothing could be done without touching upon a canonical question. These absolute religions, like Islamism and Judaism, allow no participation: if they do not reign, they call themselves persecuted. If they feel themselves protected, they become exacting, and seek to render life impossible to other worships about them.

I should depart from my plan if I recounted to you that strange struggle of which Josephus tells us, — the terror in Jerusalem, Simon Bar-Gioras, commandant in the city, John of Giscala with his assassins, master of the temple. Fanatical movements are far from excluding hate, jealousy, and defiance, from those who take part in them. Very decided and passionate men associated together ordinarily suspect each other, and in this there is a force; for reciprocal suspicion establishes terror among them, binds them as with an iron chain, hinders defections and moments of weakness. Interest creates the *coterie*. Absolute principles create division, and inspire the temptation to decimate, to expel, to kill enemies. Those who judge human affairs superficially believe that a revolution is quelled when the revolutionists "eat one another," as it is expressed. It is, on the contrary, a proof that the revolution has all its energy, that an impersonal ardor presides over it. This is nowhere more clearly seen than in the terrible drama at Jerusalem. The actors seem to have entered into the compact of death like some infernal rounds, in which, according to the belief of the middle ages, Satan was seen forming a chain to draw into a fantastic gulf numbers of men, dancing, and holding each other by the hand. So revolution allows no one to escape from the dance which it leads. Terror is behind the lukewarm. Turn by turn, exalting some, and exalted by others, they rush into the abyss. None can recede; for behind each one is a concealed sword, which, at the moment that he wishes to draw back, forces him to advance.

The strangest thing of all is that these madmen were not wholly wrong. The fanatics of Jerusalem, who affirmed that Jerusalem was eternal even while it was burning, were nearer the truth than those who regarded them as mere assassins. They deceived themselves upon the military question, but not upon the distant religious result. These troubled days point out, in fact, the moment when

Jerusalem became the spiritual capital of the world. The Apocalypse, a burning expression of the love which she inspired, has taken its place among the religious writings of humanity, and has there consecrated the image of the beloved city. Ah, how important it is never to predict the future of a saint or a villain, a fool or a sage! Jerusalem, a city of common people, would have pursued indefinitely its uninteresting history. It is because it had the incomparable honor of being the cradle of Christianity, that it was the victim of the Johns of Giscala, of the Bar-Gioras, — in appearance the scourges of their country, in reality the instruments of its apotheosis. These zealots, whom Josephus treats as brigands and assassins, were politicians of the highest order, but unskilful soldiers: still they lost heroically a country which could not be saved. They lost a material city: they established the spiritual reign of Jerusalem, sitting in her desolation far more glorious than she was in the days of Herod and of Solomon. What did these conservatives, these Sadducees, really desire? They wished something mean, — the continuation of a city of priests like Emesa, Tyane, Comane. Assuredly they did not deceive themselves when they declared that the surging enthusiasm was the ruin of the nation. Revolution and Messianism destroyed the national existence of the Jewish people; but revolution and Messianism were the true vocation of this people, — that by which they contributed to the universal civilization.

II.

THE victory of Rome was complete. A captain of our race, of our blood, a man like us, at the head of legions in whose roll, if we could read it, we should meet many of our ancestors, had come to crush the fortress of Semitism, to inflict upon the revealed, accepted law the greatest injury which it had received. It was the triumph of Roman right, or rather rational right, a creation utterly philosophical, presupposing no revelation, above the Jewish Thora, the fruit of a revelation. This right, whose roots were partly Greek, but in which the practical genius of the Latins made so fine a part, was the excellent gift which Rome brought to the vanquished in return for their independence. Each victory for Rome was a victory for right. Rome bore into the world a better principle in several respects than that of the Jews: I mean the profane state, reposing on a purely civil conception of society.

The triumph of Titus was then legitimate in many ways, and still there never was a more useless triumph. The deplorable religious nothingness of Rome rendered its victory unfruitful. This victory did not retard the progress of Judaism a single day: it did not give the religion of the empire an added chance to struggle against this redoubtable rival. The national existence of the Jewish people was lost forever; but that was a blessing. The true glory of Judaism was Christianity, about to be born. The ruin of Jerusalem and the temple was an unequalled good for Christianity.

If the reasoning of Titus according to Tacitus is correctly reported, the victorious general believed that the destruction of the temple would be the ruin of Christianity as well as that of Judaism. No one was ever more completely deceived. The Romans imagined, that, in tearing up the root, they should eradicate the shoot at the same time; but the shoot was already a shrub that lived its own life. If the temple had survived, Christianity would certainly have been arrested in its development. The surviving temple would have continued to be the centre of all Judaic works. It would always have been regarded as the most holy place of the world: pilgrims would have come there, and would there have brought their tributes. The Church of Jerusalem, grouped around by consecrated parvises, would have continued, by the strength of its primacy, to receive the homage of all the world, to persecute the Christians of the Church of Paul, to exact, that, in order to have the right to call one's self the disciple of Jesus, one should practise the circumcision, and observe the Mosaic code. All effectual propagandism would have been interdicted: letters of obedience signed at Jerusalem would have been exacted from the missionary. A centre of irrefragable authority, a patriarchate composed of a sort of college of cardinals under the presidency of men like James, pure Jews belonging to the family of Jesus, would have been established, and would have constituted an immense danger for the new-born Church. When one sees St. Paul after so many mishaps remaining always attached to the Church of Jerusalem, one understands what difficulties a rupture with these holy personages would have presented. Such a schism would have been considered as an enormity. The separation from Judaism would have been impossible; and this separation was the indispensable condition of the existence of the new religion. The mother was about to kill the child. The temple, on the contrary, once destroyed, the Christians thought no more of it: very soon, indeed, they will consider it a profane place: Jesus will be every thing to them. The Christian Church of Jerusalem was by the same stroke reduced to a secondary importance. It was re-organized around the element which made its force, the *desposyni*, the members of the family of Jesus, the sons of Clopas; but it will reign no more. This centre of hate and exclusion once destroyed, the reconciliation of the opposing parties in the Church of Jesus will become easy. Peter and Paul will be brought into accord, and the terrible duality of the new-born Christianity will cease to be a mortal sore. Lost in the depth of the interior of the Batanæa and the Hauran, the little group which attached itself to James and Clopas becomes the Ebionite sect, and slowly dies.

These relatives of Jesus were pious, tranquil, mild, modest, hard-working men, faithful to the severest precepts of Jesus concerning poverty, but at the same time very exact Jews, considering the title of "Child of Israel" before every other advantage. From the year 70 to about the year 110, they really governed the churches beyond the Jordan, and formed a sort of Christian senate. There is no need to demonstrate the immense danger which these pre-occupations, with genealogies, were to the new-born Christianity. A sort of nobility of Christianity was about to be formed. In the political order the nobility is almost a necessity to the state. Politics having elements of gross struggles which render it more material than ideal, a state is very strong only when a certain number of families has, by tradition and privilege, the duty and interest of guarding its welfare, representing and defending it. But, in the order of the ideal government, birth is noth ing: each one is valued in proportion to the truth he shows, and the good he does. The institutions which have a religious, literary, moral end, are lost, when considerations of family, caste, heredity, prevail in them. The nephews and cousins of Jesus would have ruined Christianity, if the churches of Paul had not already been strong enough to act as a counterpoise to this aristocracy, the tendency of which would have been to proclaim itself alone respectable, and to treat all converts as intruders. Some pretensions analogous to those of the Alides in Islam were established. Islamism would certainly have perished under the embarrassment caused by the family of the prophet, if the result of the struggles of the first century of the Hegira had not been to reject, upon second thought, all those who were too near the person of the prophet. The true heirs of a great man are those who continue his work, and not his relatives by blood. Considering the tradition of Jesus as his own possession, the little *coterie* of the Nazarenes, as they are called, would certainly have stifled it. Happily this narrow circle disappeared in good season: the relatives of Jesus were soon forgotten in the interior of the Hauran. They lost all importance, and left Jesus to his true family, the only one which he has recognized, — those of whom he said, "They hear the word of God, and keep it."

III.

According as the Church of Jerusalem sank, the Church of Rome rose, or, rather, a phenomenon was evidently manifested in the years which followed the victory of Titus. It was that the Church of Rome became more and more the inheritor and the substitute of the Church of Jerusalem. The spirit of the two churches was the same: what was a danger at Jerusalem became an advantage at Rome. The taste for tradition and the hierarchy, and the respect for authority, were in some sort transplanted from the parvises of the temple to the Occident. James, the brother of the Lord, had been a sort of pope at Jerusalem. Rome is about to take up the part of James. We shall have the pope at Rome. Without Titus, we should have had the pope in Jerusalem, but with this great difference, that the pope at Jerusalem would have extinguished Christianity in about one or two hundred years, while the Pope of Rome has made it the religion of the universe.

Here appears a very important person, who seems to have been the head of the Roman Church in the early years of the first century, concerning whom I am happy to find myself in accord with one of your most scholarly and enlightened critics, Mr. Lightfoot. I speak of Clement Romanus. In the penumbra in which he remains, enveloped and almost lost in the luminous dust of a beautiful far-off history, Clement is one of the grand figures of early Christianity: one would say that it was the head of an old effaced fresco of Giotto's, recognizable still from his golden aureola, and some dim features of striking purity and sweetness. One thing is beyond doubt: it is the high rank which he held in the utterly spiritual hierarchy of the church of his time, and the unequalled credit with which he sustained it. His approval made the law. All parties clung to him, and wished to shield themselves under his authority. It is probable that he was one of the most energetic agents of the grand work that was about to be accomplished: I mean the posthumous reconciliation of Peter and Paul, without which union the work of Christ could only have perished. His high personality, aggrandized by tradition, was, after that of Peter, the most holy figure of the primitive Christian Rome.

Already the idea of a certain primacy in the Church of Rome began to show itself. The right of advising the other churches and of settling their differences was accorded to this church. It is believed that like privileges had been allowed to Peter among the disciples. Now a still closer bond was established between Peter and Rome. In the time of Clement, great dissensions divided the Church at Corinth. The Roman Church, being applied to in these troubles, replied by an epistle, which has been preserved to us. The epistle is anonymous; but a very ancient tradition teaches that Clement was the author of it. The Church at Corinth had changed but little since St. Paul. It had the same proud, disputant, feeble spirit. It is evident that the principal opposition to the hierarchy was found in this Greek spirit, always mobile, because it was always full of life, undisciplined (and for my part I like it), not knowing how to form a flock from a crowd. The women and the children were in full revolt. Some superior doctors imagined that they possessed a profound sense in every thing, and mystic secrets analogous to the gift of tongues and the discernment of spirits. Those who were honored with these supernatural gifts scorned the ancients, and aspired to replace them. Corinth had a respectable presbytery, which, however, did not receive the highest mysticism. The advanced pretenders cast it in the shade, and put themselves in its place. Some of the *presbyteri* were even dismissed. The struggle between the established hierarchy and personal revelations began, and this struggle fills the history of the Church; the privileged soul complaining, that, in spite of the favors with which it is honored, a gross clergy, wanting in spiritual life, dominates it officially. We see that this was the heresy of individual mysticism, maintaining the rights of the spirit against authority, pretending to rise above common mortals and the ordinary clergy by right of its direct intercourse with divinity.

The Roman Church was always the church of order, of subordination, and of rule. Its fundamental principle was that humility and submission were of more value than the most sublime gifts. Its epistle is the first manifestation in the Christian Church of the principle of authority.

A few years since, there was much surprise when a French archbishop, then a senator, said in the Tribune, "My clergy is my regiment." Clement had said this before him. Order and obedience were the supreme laws of the family and the church. "Let us consider the soldiers who serve under our sovereigns. With what order, what punctuality, what submission, they obey their commands: all are not prefects, nor tribunes, nor centurions; but each one in his rank executes the orders of the emperor and of his chiefs. The great cannot exist without the small, nor the small without the great. In every thing there is a mingling of diverse elements, and by this mingling all advances. Let us take, for example, our bodies. The head is nothing without the feet; the feet are nothing without the head. The smallest of our organs are necessary, and serve the whole body: all conspire, and obey the same principle of subordination for the preservation of the whole."

The history of the ecclesiastical hierarchy is the history of a triple abdication; the community of the faithful first placing all its powers in the hands of the ancients, or *presbyteri;* the presbyteral body at length delegating its authority to one person who was the *episcopos;* then the *episcopi* of the Latin Church recognized as their head one of themselves, who became the pope. This last progress, if we may call it so, was not accomplished until our time. The creation of the episcopate, on the contrary, was the work of the second century. The absorption of the church by the *presbyteri* was accomplished before the year 100. In the Epistle of Clement Romanus it is not yet with the episcopate, but with the presbytery, that he deals. We find there no trace of a *presbyteros* superior to the others, and entitled to dethrone them; but the author proclaims positively that the presbytery and the clergy are above the people. The apostles, in establishing churches, chose through the inspiration of the Spirit the "bishops and the deacons of the future believers." The power emanating from the apostles has been transmitted by regular succession. No church has then the right to dethrone its seniors. The privilege of the rich is nothing in the church. Accordingly, those who are favored with mystic gifts, instead of believing themselves above the hierarchy, should be the more submissive. This involves the great problem, "Who exists in the church? Is it the people? Is it the clergy? Is it inspiration?" This problem was already given in the time of St. Paul, who resolved it in the true manner by mutual charity. One epistle trenches upon the question in the sense of pure Catholicism. The apostolic title is every thing: the right of the people is reduced to nothing. We may then safely assert that Catholicism had its origin at Rome, since the Church of Rome laid down its first rules. Prescience pertains to spiritual gifts, to science and distinction: it belongs to the hierarchy, to the powers transmitted through the medium of the canonical ordination, which attaches itself to the apostles by an unbroken chain. The free church as Christ conceived it, and as St. Paul also regarded it, was a Utopia which held nothing for the future. Evangelical liberty had destroyed it; and it was not realized, that, with the hierarchy uniformity and death would come in time.

IV.

Clement had probably not seen either Peter or Paul. His great practical sense showed him that the salvation of the Christian Church demanded the reconciliation of the two founders. Did he influence the author of the Acts which represent to us this reconciliation as accomplished, and with whom he seems to have had some intercourse, or did these two pious souls spontaneously fall into accord on account of the bias which he had given to Christian opinion? We are ignorant for want of proofs. One thing is sure, the reconciliation of Peter and Paul was a Roman work. Rome had two churches,— one coming from Peter, the other from Paul. Those numerous converts who came to Jesus — some through the school of Peter, and some through that of Paul — were tempted to exclaim, "What! Are there, then, two Christs?" It was necessary to be able to reply, "No: Peter and Paul understand each other perfectly: the Christianity of one is the Christianity of the other." Perhaps (this is an ingenious hypothesis of M. Strauss) a light cloud was introduced for this purpose into the evangelical legend of the miraculous fishing. According to the recital of Luke, the nets of Peter would not contain the multitudes of fish which could easily have been taken; Peter was obliged to make a sign to his co-workers to come to his aid. A second bark (Paul and his friends) was filled as the first, and the fishing of the kingdom of God was superabundant.

The life of the apostles begins to become obscure. All those who have seen them have disappeared: most of them left no writings. One had entire liberty to embroider on this virgin canvas still. Friends and enemies profited by the unknown to set up arguments in support of their theses, and to satisfy their hates. Towards the year 130, that is to say about sixty-six years after the death of the apostles, a vast Ebionite legend was produced at Rome, and designated by the title of the preaching, or the travels, of Peter. The missions of the chief of the apostles were recounted there, principally those along the coast of Phœnicia; the conversions which he had made; above all, his struggles against the great anti-Christ, Simon the Magician, who was at this epoch the spectre of the Christian conscience. But frequently under this abhorred name another person was concealed: it was the false apostle Paul, the enemy of the law, the veritable destroyer of the Church. The true Church was that at Jerusalem, presided over by James, the brother of the Lord. No apostolate was of any value, if it could not show letters emanating from this central college. Paul had none: therefore he was an intruder. He was the "man enemy," who came behind to sow the tares in the steps of the true sower. With what fury Peter gave the denial to his impostures, to his false allegations of personal revelations, his ascension to the third heaven, his pretension of knowing about Jesus some things which the hearers of the gospel had not understood, the exaggerated manner in which he and his disciples interpreted the divinity of Jesus!

These strange ideas of half ignorant sectaries would have been without consequences outside of Rome; but every thing which related to Peter assumed importance in the capital of the world. In spite of its heresies, " The Preachings of Peter" had much interest for the orthodox. The primacy of Peter was there proclaimed. St. Paul was thus injured; but a few retouches extenuated what was shocking in these attacks. Several attempts were made to diminish the peculiarities of the new book, and adapt it to the Catholics. This mode of remodelling books to suit the sect to which one belonged was the order of the day. Little by little the force of things was understood: all sensible men saw that there was safety for the work of Jesus only in the perfect reconciliation of the two heads of the Christian doctrine. Paul had, even in the sixth century, some bitter enemies: he had always some enthusiastic followers like Marcion. Outside of these obstinate men of the right and left, there was a union of the moderate masses, who, before their Christianism in one of the schools, fully recognized the right of the other to be called Christian. James, the partisan of absolute Judaism, was sacrificed, although he had been the true chief of the circumcision. Peter, who was much less objectionable to the disciples of Paul, was preferred before him. James retained no devoted partisans outside of the Judean-Christians.

It is difficult to say who gained the most in this reconciliation. The concessions came principally from the side of Paul: all Paul's disciples received the others without difficulty, while those of Peter repulsed the followers of Paul. But concessions usually come from the strong. In truth, each day confirmed Paul's victory.

Each Gentile convert weighted the balance on his side. Outside of Syria, the Judean-Christians were swallowed up by the wave of new converts. The churches of Paul prospered: they had good judgment, solidity of mind, and some pecuniary resources which the others had not. The Ebionite churches, on the contrary, grew poorer each day. The money of the churches of Paul was spent in the support of some glorious poor men, who were unable to earn any thing, but who possessed the traditional life of the primitive spirit. The elevated piety and severe manners of these last were admired by the Christian communities of Pagan origin, who imitated and assimilated themselves to these customs. It soon happened that no distinction was manifest: the sweet and conciliatory spirit of St. Luke and Clement Romanus prevailed. The compact of peace was sealed. It was agreed that Peter had converted the first-fruits of the Gentiles, that he had first absolved them from the yoke of the law. It was admitted that Peter and Paul had been the two heads, the founders of the Church of Rome; Peter and Paul became the halves of an inseparable couple, — two luminaries, like the sun and moon. What one taught, the other taught also. They had always been in accord: they had opposed the same enemies, had been victims of Simon the Magician. At Rome they lived like brothers; the Church of Rome was their common work. The supremacy of this church was established for ages.

Thus, from the reconciliation of these parties, the settlement of these primitive struggles, there came forth a grand unity, — the Catholic Church, the Church of Peter and of Paul, a stranger to the rivalries which had marked the first century.

It was, above all, the death of the two apostles which pre-occupied the parties, and gave an opportunity for the most diverse combinations. The tissue of tradition grew in this respect, by an instinctive travail, almost as imperious as that which had presided at the construction of the legend of Jesus. The end of the life of Peter and of Paul was commanded *à priori*. It was maintained that Christ had predicted the martyrdom of Peter, as he had announced the death of the sons of Zebedee. The need was felt of associating in death the two persons who had been reconciled by force. It was hoped, and perhaps this was not far from right, that they died together, or at least as the consequence of the same event. The places which were believed to have been sanctified by this bloody drama were early fixed upon, and consecrated by *memoriæ*. In each case, whatever the people desired came in the end to be true. Tradition makes history, retrospectively, as it ought to have been, and as it never is. Not long ago the portraits of Victor Emmanuel and Pius IX. hung side by side in every frequented place in Italy; and the people desired that these two men, who represented principles whose reconciliation was generally considered necessary to Italy, should be in reality completely united. If, in our time, such views impose themselves on history, it will one day appear, in documents reputed to be serious, that Victor Emmanuel and Pius IX. (probably Garibaldi will be added) met each other secretly, understood and loved each other. During the middle ages, at different times, similar attempts were made to appease the hatreds of the Dominicans and Franciscans; to prove that the founders of these two orders were two brothers living together in the most affectionate intercourse; that at first their rules were the same; and that St. Dominic girded himself with the cord of St. Francis.

Concerning Peter and Paul, the increase of the legend was rich and rapid. Rome and all its environs, above all the way to Ostia, were full of souvenirs which were pretended to be connected with the last days of the two apostles. A crowd of touching circumstances; the flight of Peter; the vision of Jesus bearing his cross, *iterum crucifigi;* the final adieu of Peter and Paul; the meeting of Peter with his wife; Paul at the Salvian waters; Plautilla sending the handkerchief which bound her hair to bandage the eyes of Paul, — all this presented a beautiful ensemble, to which was only wanting an ingenuous and skilful writer. It was too late; the vein of the first Christian literature was spent; the serenity of the narrator of the Acts was lost; his voice was raised no more in story or in romance. It is impossible to choose between a crowd of equally apocryphal writings: in vain one seeks to shield these recitals with the most venerable names (pseudo-Linus, pseudo-Marcellus); the Roman legend of Peter and Paul remains always in a sporadic state. It was more often recounted by the pious guides than seriously read. It was a local affair: no text concerning it has been consecrated and made authoritative for reading in the churches.

Many among you, ladies and gentlemen, will go to Rome, or will return there. Ah, well! if you preserve any good remembrance of these conferences, go, in memory of me, to the Salvian waters, *alle tre fontane*, to St. Paul-without-the-Walls. It is one of the most beautiful parts of the Roman Campagna, — deserted, damp, green, and sad. There, in a deep depression in the soil, crowned by those grand horizontal lines, disturbed by no living detail, — there are some clear and cold springs. The fever and mouldiness of the tomb are inhaled there. Some Trappists are there established, conscientiously practising their religious suicide. When you are there, sit down a moment, not too long (one quickly catches the fever there), and, while the Trappists give you to drink the water which gushes from the three bounds which the head of Paul made, think of him who came here to talk of these legends with you, and to whom you have listened with so much courtesy and kind attention.

FOURTH CONFERENCE,

London, April 14, 1880.

ROME,
THE CAPITAL OF CATHOLICISM.

FOURTH CONFERENCE.

ROME, THE CAPITAL OF CATHOLICISM.

Ladies and Gentlemen, — It is plain that the importance of the churches in the primitive Christian community was in proportion to their apostolic nobility. The guaranty of orthodoxy was in the succession of the bishops, by which the great churches were linked to the apostles. A direct line appeared to afford a very strong assurance of conformity of doctrine, and it was jealously maintained. Now, what can be said of a church founded by both Peter and Paul? It is clear that such a church ought to endure in order to have a veritable superiority over others. The *chef-d'œuvre* of the competency of the Roman Church was the establishment of this superiority. That once assured, the ecclesiastical destiny of Rome was established. When this city should have cast off her secular character, she would have another, — a sacred capacity, corresponding to that of Jerusalem.

She would know how to confiscate to her profit this Christianity which she had so cruelly combated, — so much had humanity suffered, to escape from those whom fate had designed for this great secular task, *regere imperio populos!*

Under Antonine and Marcus Aurelius, Rome reached its highest grandeur; its rule of the whole world seemed to be undisputed; no cloud could be seen upon its horizon. The emigration from the provinces, above all from the Orient, was augmented rather than lessened. The Greek-speaking population was larger than it had ever been. All who desired a place in the world aspired to come to Rome: nothing was sanctioned until it had received the stamp of this universal exposition of the products of the entire universe.

The centre of a future catholic orthodoxy was evidently there. The well-developed germ of the Papacy existed under Antonine. The Church of Rome showed itself more and more indifferent to those crude Gnostic speculations which occupied some minds filled with the intellectual activity of the Greeks, but tainted with the reveries of the Orient. The organization of Christian society was the principal labor at Rome. This extraordinary city applied to this object the energetic moral strength and the practical genius which she has employed in the most diverse causes. Careless of speculation, decidedly hostile to dogmatic innovations, she presided there, — a mistress already trained by all the changes which had been brought about in discipline and in the hierarchy.

I.

From the year 120 to 130 the Episcopate was elaborated in the Christian Church, and the creation of the Episcopate was eminently a Roman work. All *ecclesiæ* imply a little hierarchy,—a bureau as it is called to-day,—a president, some assessors, and a small staff of men in its service. Democratic associations are careful that these functions shall be limited as far as possible as to power and duration; but from this arises that precarious something which has prevented any democratic association from outlasting the circumstances which have created it. The Jewish synagogues have had more continuity, although the synagogical body has never come to be a clergy. This is the result of the subordinate place which Judaism has held during several centuries: the pressure from without has counteracted the effects of internal divisions. If the Christian Church had been left with the same absence of directorship, it would doubtless have missed its destiny.

If its ecclesiastical powers had continued to be regarded as emanating from the Church itself, it would have lost all its hieratic and theocratic character. It was written, on the contrary, that a clergy should monopolize the Christian Church, and substitute themselves for it. Acting as its spokesman, presenting itself as having the sole power of attorney in every thing, this clergy will be its strength, and at the same time its gnawing worm, — the principal cause of its future falls.

I repeat, that history has no example of a more complete transformation than that which occurred in the government of the Christian Church about the time of Hadrian and Antonine. What happened in the Christian Church will happen in any association in which the subordinates could resign in favor of the bureau, and that again in favor of the president; so that afterwards the subordinates and the seniors would have no deliberative voice nor influence, nor any control in the management of the funds, and the president would be able to say, "I alone, I, am the association." The *presbyteri* (seniors) or *episcopi* (superintending officers) became very soon the only representatives of the Church; and almost immediately another still more important revolution took place. Among the *presbyteri* or *episcopi*, there had been one, who, through the habit of occupying the principal seat, absorbed the power of the others, and became pre-eminently the *episcopos* or the *presbyteros*. The form of worship contributed powerfully to the establishment of this unity. The eucharistic act could only be celebrated by one person, and gave to the celebrant an extreme importance. That *episcopos*, with a surprising rapidity, became the head of the presbytery, and, consequently, the entire Church. His *cathedra* was placed apart, and, having the form of an arm-chair, became the seat of honor, the symbol of primacy. From this time, each church has but one chief *presbyteros*, who is thus called to the exclusion of the other *episcopi*. Beside this bishop, there were deacons, widows, and a council of *presbyteri:* but the great step has been taken; the bishop is the sole successor of the prophets, his associates have disappeared. Apostolic authority, reputed as transmitted by the laying-on of hands, suppressed the authority of the community. The bishops of the various churches soon placed themselves in communication with the others, and formed of the Universal Church a sort of oligarchy, which held assemblies, censured its members, decided questions of faith, and was in itself a true sovereign power. On one side, the shepherds; on the other, the flock. Primitive equality no longer existed: in fact, it had endured but a single day. The Church, however, was only an instrument in the hands of those who guided her; and these held their power, not from the community, but from the spiritual inheritance of a transmission claiming to date back to the apostles in a continuous line. It is evident that the representative system will never be in any degree whatever the law of the Christian Church.

It was the Episcopate, without the intervention

of civil power, with no support from the tribunals, which thus established order above liberty in a society originally founded upon individual inspiration. This is why the Ebionites, who had no Episcopate, had also no idea of Catholicity. At first sight, the work of Jesus was not made to last. Founded upon a belief in the destruction of the world, which, as years rolled on, was proved an error, it seemed that his congregation could only dissolve in anarchy. The prophetic book, the *charismes*, the speaking of tongues, individual inspiration, were no more than were necessary to bring all again into the proportions of a common chapel. Individual inspiration created, but immediately destroyed what it created. After liberty, law is necessary. The work of Jesus might be considered as saved the day in which it was admitted that the Church has a direct power, a power representing that of Jesus. Since then the Church dominates the individual, drawing him to her bosom through his need. Inspiration passes from the individual to the community. The clergy is the dispenser of all pardons, the intermediary between God and the faithful. Obedience, first to the Church, then to the bishop, becomes the highest duty. Innovation is the sign of error: schism, henceforth, will be for the Christian the worst of crimes.

In a certain regard one may say that this was a

decadence, a diminution of that spontaneity which had been eminently creative until now. It was evident that ecclesiastical forms were about to absorb, to stifle, the work of Jesus, that all free manifestations of Christian life would soon be arrested. Under the censure of the Episcopate, the speaking of tongues, prophecy, the creation of legends, the making of new sacred books, would soon become withered powers, the *charismes* would be reduced to official sacraments. In another sense, however, such a transformation was the essential condition of the strength of humanity. And, moreover, the centralization of powers became necessary when churches were more numerous: intercourse between these little pious societies would be impossible, unless they had representatives appointed to act for them. It is undeniable, moreover, that, without the Episcopate, the churches, re-united for a time by the souvenirs of Jesus, would gradually have been dispersed. The divergences of opinion, the difference in the turn of imagination, and, above all, the rivalries, and the unsatisfied *amours-propres*, would have operated by their infinite effects of disunion and disintegration. Christianity would have expired at the end of three or four centuries, like Mithracism and so many other sects which were not allowed to endure. Democracy is sometimes eminently creative; but it is upon the condition that the democracy comes forth from conservative institutions which prevent the revolutionary fever from prolonging itself indefinitely.

Here was the greatest miracle of the new Christianity. It drew order, hierarchy, authority, and obedience from the free subjection of desires: it organized the crowd; it disciplined anarchy. What does this miracle accomplish other than to strike at the pretended derogations to the laws of physical nature? The spirit of Jesus strongly inoculated in his disciples that spirit of sweetness, of abnegation, of forgetfulness of the present; that unique pursuit of interior joys which kills ambition; that strong preference given to childhood; those words repeated without ceasing, as from Jesus, "Whoever is first among you, let him be the servant of all." The influence of the apostles was not less in that direction. The apostles lived and ruled after their death. The idea that the head of the Church held his command under the members of the Church who had elected him never once occurs in the literature of this time. The Church thus escaped through the supernatural origin of its power, that element of decay which exists in delegated authority. A legislative and executive authority may come from the people; but sacraments and dispensations of celestial pardons have nothing in common with universal suffrage. Such privileges come from heaven, or, according to the Christian formula, from Jesus Christ, the source of all pardon and of all good.

The religion of Jesus thus became something solid and consistent. The great danger of Gnosticism, which was to divide Christianity into numberless sects, was exorcised. The word "Catholic Church" resounded everywhere, as the name of that great body which would thenceforth survive the ages unbroken. The character of this catholicity is already seen. The Montanists are regarded as sectarian; the Marcionites are convinced of the falseness of the apostolic doctrine; the different Gnostic schools are more and more driven from the bosom of the general church. Something had arisen which was neither Montanism, nor Marcionism, nor Gnosticism; which was Christianity, not sectarian, — the Christianity of the majority of bishops, resisting sects, and using them all, having, if you will, only negative characters, but preserved by these negative characters from the pietist aberrations, and from dissolving rationalism. Christianity, like all parties who wish to live, disciplines itself, and restrains its own excesses. It unites to mystical exaltation a fund of good sense and moderation which will kill Millenarism, Charisms, Glossolaly, and all the primitive phenomenal spirits. A handful of excited men, like the Montanists, running into martyrdom, discouraging penitence, condemning marriage, are not the Church. The *juste milieu* triumphs. Radicals of any sort will never be allowed to destroy the work of Jesus. The Church is always of a medium opinion: it belongs to all the world, and is not the privilege of an aristocracy. The pietist aristocracy of the Phrygian sects and the speculative aristocracy of the Gnostics are equally stripped of their pretensions.

In the midst of the enormous variety of opinions which fill the first Christian age, the Catholic opinion constitutes a sort of standard. It was not necessary to reason with the heretic in order to convince him. It was sufficient to show him that he was not in communion with the Catholic Church, with the grand churches which trace the succession of their bishops to the apostles. *Quod semper, quod ubique* became the absolute rule of truth. The argument of prescription to which Tertullian gave such eloquent force reviews all the Catholic controversy. To prove to any one that he was an innovator, a disturber, was to prove that he was wrong, — an insufficient rule, since, by a singular irony of fate, the doctor himself who developed this method of refutation in so imperious a manner, Tertullian, died a heretic.

Correspondence between the churches was an early custom. Circular letters from the heads of the great churches, read on Sunday in the reunions of the faithful, were a sort of continuation of the apostolic literature. The ecclesiastical province, questioning the precedency of the great churches, appeared in germ. The Church, like the synagogue and the mosque, is essentially a citadel. Christianity, like Judaism and Islamism, is a religion of cities. The countryman, the *paganus*, will be the last resistance which Christianity will encounter. The few rural Christians came to the church of the neighboring city. The Roman municipality thus enclosed the church. Among the cities, the *civitas*, the grand city, was alone a veritable church, with an *episcopos*. The small city was in ecclesiastical dependence on the great city. This primacy of the great cities was an important fact. The great city once converted, the small city and the country followed the movement. The diocese was thus the unity of the conglomerate Christians. As for the ecclesiastical province, it corresponded to the Roman province: the divisions of worship of Rome and Augustus were the secret law which ruled all. Those cities which had a flamen, or *archiereus*, are those which later had an archbishop: the *flamen civitatis* became the bishop. After the third century, the flamen held the rank in the city which was later that of the bishop in the diocese. Thus it happened that the ecclesiastical geography of a country was very nearly the geography of the same country in the Roman epoch. The picture of the bishops and the archbishops is that of the ancient *civitates*, according to their line of subordination. The empire was as the mould in which the new religion was formed. The interior framework, the outlines, the hierarchical divisions, were those of the empire. The ancient archives of the Roman administration, and the church-registers of the middle ages, and even those of our own day, are nearly the same thing.

Thus the grand organisms which have become so essential a part of the moral and political life of European nations were all created by those *naïve* and sincere Christians, whose faith has become inseparable from the moral culture of humanity. The Episcopate under Marcus Aurelius was fully ripe: the Papacy existed in germ. Œcumenical councils were impossible. The Christian Empire alone could authorize great assemblies; but the provincial synod was used in the affairs of the Montanists and of the Passover. The bishop of the capital of the province was allowed to preside without contest.

II.

ROME was the place in which the grand idea of Catholicity was conceived. Rome became each day more and more the capital of Christianity, and replaced Jerusalem as the religious centre of humanity. Its church had a generally recognized precedence over others. All doubtful questions which disturbed the Christian conscience demanded an arbitration, if not a solution, at Rome. This very defective reasoning was used, — that, since Christ had made Cephas the corner-stone of his church, this privilege ought to extend to his successors. By an unequalled stroke, the Church of Rome had succeeded in making itself at the same time the Church of Peter and the Church of Paul, a new mythical duality, replacing that of Romulus and Remus. The Bishop of Rome became the bishop of bishops, the one who admonished others. Rome proclaims its right (a dangerous right) to excommunicate those who do not entirely agree with her. The poor Artemonites (a sort of anticipated Arians) had much to complain of in the injustice of the fate which made them heretics; while, even until Victor, all the Church of Rome thought with them; but they were not heard. From this point, the Church of Rome placed itself above history. The spirit which in 1870 could proclaim the infallibility of the Pope might see itself reflected at the end of the second century by certain clear indications. The writing made at Rome about 180, of which the Roman fragment known as the "*Canon de Muratori*" makes a part, shows us Rome already regulating the canon of the churches, making the passion of Peter the basis of Catholicity, and repulsing equally Montanism and Gnosticism.

Irenæus refutes all heresies by the faith of this church, "the grandest, the most ancient, the most illustrious, which possesses by continuous succession the true tradition of the apostles Peter and Paul; to which, on account of its primacy, all the rest of the Church should have recourse."

One material cause contributed much to that pre-eminence which most of the churches recognized in the Church of Rome. This Church was extremely rich: its goods, skilfully administered, served to succor and propagate other churches. The heretics condemned to the mines received a subsidy from it: the common treasury was in a certain sense at Rome. The Sunday collection, practised continually in the Roman Church, was probably already established. A marvellous spirit of tradition animated this little community, in which Judæa, Greece, and Latium seemed to have confounded their very different gifts, in view of a prodigious future. While the Jewish Monotheism furnished the immovable base of the new formation, while Greece continued through Gnosticism its work of free speculation, Rome attached itself with an astonishing readiness to the work of the government. All its authorities and artifices served well for that. Politics recoils not before fraud. Now, politics had already taken up its home in the most secret councils of the Church of Rome. Some veins of apocryphal literature, constantly refilled, sometimes under the name of the apostles, sometimes under that of apostolic personages, such as Clement and Hermas, were received with confidence to the limits of the Christian world on account of the guaranty of Rome.

This precedence of the Church of Rome continued to increase up to the third century. The bishops of Rome showed a rare competency, evading theological questions, but always in the first rank in matters of organization and administration. The tradition of the Roman Church passes for the most ancient of all. Pope Cornelius took the lead in the matter of substitution. This was particularly seen in the dismissal of the bishops of Italy, and the appointment of their successors. Rome was also the central authority of the churches of Africa.

This authority was already excessive, and showed itself above all in the affair of the Passover. This question was much more important than it appears to us. In the early times all Christians continued to make the Jewish Passover their principal feast. They celebrated this feast on the same day as the Jews, — on the 14th of Nisan, upon whatever day of the week it happened to fall. Persuaded, according to the account of all the old gospels, that Jesus, the evening before his death, had eaten the Passover with his disciples, they regarded such a solemnity as a commemoration of the last supper, rather than as a memorial of the resurrection. As Christianity became more and more separated from Judaism, such a manner of regarding it was very much questioned. At first a new tradition was promulgated, — that Jesus, being about to die, had not eaten the Passover, but had died the very day of the Jewish feast, thus constituting himself the Pascal Lamb. Moreover, this purely Jewish feast wounded the Christian conscience, especially in the churches of Paul. The great feast of the Christians, the resurrection of Jesus, occurred in any case the Sunday after the Jewish Passover. According to this idea, the feast was celebrated the Sunday which followed the Friday after the 14th of Nisan.

In Rome this custom prevailed, at least since the pontificates of Xystus and Telesphorus (about 120). In Asia there were great divisions. The conservatives, like Polycarp, Meliton, and all the ancient school, believed that the old Jewish custom conformed to the first Gospels and to the usage of the apostles John and Philip. This was the object of the voyage to Rome which Polycarp undertook about the year 154, under the Pope Anicetus. The interview between Polycarp and Anicetus was very cordial. The discussion of certain points appears to have been sharp, but they understood each other. Polycarp was not able to persuade Anicetus to renounce a practice which had been that of the bishops of Rome before his time. Anicetus, on the other hand, hesitated when Polycarp told him that he governed himself according to the rule of John and the other apostles, with whom he had lived on a familiar footing. The two religious leaders remained in full communion with each other; and Anicetus showed Polycarp an almost unprecedented honor. In fact he desired that Polycarp, in the Assembly of the Faithful at Rome, should pronounce, in his stead and in his presence, the words of the eucharistic consecration. These ardent men were full of too lofty a sentiment to rest the unity of their souls upon the uniformity of rites and exterior observances.

Later, unhappily, Rome took the stand of insisting upon its right. About the year 196 the question was more exciting than ever. The churches of Asia persisted in their old usage. Rome, always enthusiastic for unity, wished to coerce them. Upon the invitation of Pope Victor, convocations of bishops were held: a vast correspondence was exchanged. But the bishops of Asia, strong in the tradition of two apostles and of so many illustrious men, would not submit. The old Polycrates, Bishop of Ephesus, wrote in their name a very sharp letter to Victor and to the Church of Rome. The incredible design which Victor conceived on account of the acrimony of this letter proves that the Papacy was already born, and well born. He pretended to excommunicate, to separate from the Universal Church, the most illustrious province, because it had not bent its traditions before the Roman discipline. He published a decree by virtue of which Asia was placed under the ban of the Christian community. But the other bishops opposed this violent measure, and recalled Victor to charity. St. Irenæus, in particular, who, through the necessity of the country in which he lived, had accepted for himself and his churches in Gaul the Occidental custom, could not support the thought that the mother-churches of Asia, to which he felt himself bound in the depths of his soul, should be separated from the body of the Universal Church. He energetically persuaded Victor from the excommunication of the churches which held to the traditions of their fathers, and recalled to him the examples of his more tolerant predecessors. This act of rare good sense prevented the schism of the Orient and the Occident from occurring in the second century. Irenæus wrote to the bishops on all sides, and the question remained open to the churches of Asia.

In one sense, the process which brought about the debate was of more importance than the debate itself. By reason of this difference, the Church was brought to a clearer idea of its organization. And first it was evident that the laity were no longer any thing. The bishops alone handled questions, and promulgated their opinions. The bishops collected together in provincial synods, over which the bishop of the capital of the province presided (the archbishop of the future), or, at times, the oldest bishop. The synodal assembly came out with a letter, which was sent to other churches. This was then like an attempt at federative organization, — an attempt to resolve questions by means of provincial assemblies, presided over by bishops agreeing among themselves. Later, questions concerning the presiding over synods and the hierarchy of the Church sought solution in the documents of this great debate. Among all the churches, that of Rome appeared to have a particular initiative right. But that initiative was far from being synonymous with infallibility; for Eusebius declares that he read the letters in which the bishops severely blamed the conduct of Victor.

III.

AUTHORITY, gentlemen, loves authority. The authoritaires, as we say to-day, in the most diverse ranks, extend the hand to each other. Men as conservative as the leaders of the Church of Rome must be strongly tempted to favor public force, the effect of which is often for good, as they must admit. This tendency had been manifest since the first days of Christianity. Jesus had laid down the rule. The image of the money was for him the supreme criterion of its lawfulness, beyond which there was nothing to seek. In the height of the reign of Nero, St. Paul wrote, "Let every soul be subject unto the higher powers. For there is no power but of God: the powers that be are ordained of God. Whosoever, therefore, resisteth the power, resisteth the ordinance of God." Some years later, Peter, or the person who wrote in his name the Epistle known as the First of Peter, expresses himself in an identical manner. Clement was an equally devoted subject of the Roman Empire.

In fine, one of the traits of St. Luke (according to my idea there was a bond between St. Luke and the spirit of the church at Rome) is his respect of the imperial authority, and the precautions which he took not to injure it. The author of the Acts evaded every thing which would present the Romans as the enemies of Christ. On the contrary, he seeks to show, that, under many circumstances, they defended St. Paul and the Christians against the Jews. Never a disparaging word against the civil magistrates. Luke loved to show how the Roman functionaries were favorable to the new religion, sometimes even embracing it; and how Roman justice was equitable, and superior to the passions of the local powers. He insists upon the advantages which Paul owed to his title of Roman citizen. If he ends his recital with the arrival of Paul at Rome, it is perhaps in order not to recount the monstrosities of Nero.

Without doubt, there were in other parts of the empire devoted Christians who sympathized entirely with the anger of the Jews, and dreamed only of the destruction of the idolatrous city which they identified with Babylon. Such were the authors of apocalypses and sibylline writings. But the faithful of the great churches were of quite a different way of thinking. In 70, the Church of Jerusalem, with a sentiment more Christian than patriotic, left the revolutionary city, and sought peace beyond the Jordan. In the revolt of Barkokébas, the division was still more pronounced. Not a single Christian was willing to take part in this attempt of blind despair. St. Justin in his Apologies never combats the principle of empire. He desired that the empire should examine the Christian doctrine, approve and countersign it in some way, and condemn those who calumniated it. The most learned doctor of the time of Marcus Aurelius, Meliton, Bishop of Sardis, made still more decided advances, and undertook to show that there is always in Christianity something to recommend it to a true Roman. In his Treaty upon Truth, preserved in Syriac, Meliton expresses himself in the same way as a bishop of the fourth century, explaining to one Theodosius that his first duty is to establish by his authority the triumph of truth (without telling us, alas! by what sign one recognizes truth). Let the empire become Christian, and the persecuted of to-day would find that the interference of the state in the domain of conscience is perfectly legitimate.

The system of the apologists, so warmly sustained by Tertullian, according to which the good emperors favored Christianity, and the bad ones persecuted it, was already full blown. "Born together," said they, "Christianity and the empire have grown up together, and prospered together." Their interests, their sufferings, their fortunes, their future, — all was in common. The apologists were advocates; and advocates in all orders resemble each other. They have arguments for every situation and all tastes. Nearly a hundred and fifty years rolled on before these sweet and half sincere invitations were understood. But the only impression they made in the time of Marcus Aurelius upon the mind of one of the most enlightened leaders of the Church was as a prognostic of the future. Christianity and the empire will become reconciled. They are made for each other. The shade of Meliton will tremble with joy when the empire becomes Christian, and the emperor takes in hand the cause of truth.

Thus the Church already took more than one step toward empire. Through politeness, without doubt, but only as a very legitimate consequence of his principles, Meliton does not allow that an emperor can give an unjust order. It was easy to believe that certain emperors had not been absolutely opposed to Christianity. It is pleasant to relate that Tiberius had proposed to place Jesus in the rank of the gods: it was the senate which objected. The decided preference of Christianity for power where it hopes for favors is already very transparent. It is shown, contrary to all truth, that Hadrian and Antonine sought to repair the evil done by Nero and Domitian. Tertullian and his generation say the same thing of Marcus Aurelius. Tertullian doubted, it is true, whether one could be at the same time a Cæsar and a Christian; but this incompatibility a century later struck no one, and Constantine proved that Meliton of Sardis was a very sagacious man when he discerned so well — a century and a half in advance, seeing through the proconsular persecutions — the possibility of a Christian Empire.

The hatred of Christianity and of the empire was that of men who must one day love them. Under the Severi, the language of the Church remained plaintive and tender, as it had been under the Antonines. The apologists affixed a species of legitimism, a pretension that the Church had always from the first saluted the emperor. "There were never among us," said Tertullian, "partisans of Cassius, partisans of Albinus, partisans of Niger." Foolish illusion! Certainly the revolt of Avidius Cassius against Marcus Aurelius was a political crime, and the Christians did well not to be involved in it. As for Severus, Albinus, and Niger, it was success that decided between them; and the Church had no other merit in attaching itself to Severus than that of seeing clearly who would the be strongest. This pretended worship of legitimacy was in truth only the worship of a fixed fact. The principle of St. Paul bore fruit: "All power comes from God: he who holds the sword holds it from God for good."

This correct attitude in regard to power clung to exterior necessities as much as to the principles which the Church had received from its founders. The Church was already a powerful association. It was essentially conservative. It needed order and legal guaranties. This was admirably shown in the act of Paul of Samos, Bishop of Antioch, under Aurelian. The Bishop of Antioch had become a powerful personage at this epoch. The goods of the Church were in his keeping: a crowd of men lived on his favors. Paul was a brilliant man, somewhat mystical, worldly, a great secular lord, seeking to render Christianity acceptable to men of the world and authority. The Pietists, as might be expected, considered him heretical, and dismissed him. Paul resisted, and refused to quit the Episcopal house. See into what the most exalted sects are led! They were in possession, and who could decide a question of proprietorship and possession, if not the civil authority. Aurelian, about this time, passed on his way towards Antioch; and the question was referred to him. Here was seen this original spectacle of an infidel sovereign and persecutor deputed to decide which was the true bishop. Aurelian showed under these circumstances remarkably good sense for a layman. He examined the correspondence of the two bishops, took note as to which was in relation with Rome and Italy, and decided that he was the true Bishop of Antioch.

Aurelian made some objections to the theological reasoning used on this occasion; but one fact was evident: it was, that Christianity could not live without the empire, and that the empire, on the other hand, could not do better than adopt Christianity as its religion. The world desired a religion of congregations, of churches, or of synagogues and chapels, — a religion in which the essence of the worship should be re-union, association, and fraternity. Christianity answered to all these conditions. Its admirable worship, its well-organized clergy, assured its future.

Several times in the third century this historical necessity fell short of realization. This is seen most plainly under those Syrian emperors whom their quality of foreigners and base origin placed beyond prejudices, and who, in spite of their vices, inaugurated a largeness of ideas and a tolerance hitherto unknown. Those Syrian women of Emesa, — Julia Domna, Julia Mæsa, Julia Mammæa, Julia Soemia, — beautiful, intelligent, perfectly fearless, and held by no tradition or social law, hesitated at nothing. They did what Roman women would never have dared. They entered the Senate, deliberated there, and governed the empire effectively, dreaming of Semiramis and Nitocris. The Roman worship seemed cold and insignificant to them. Not being bound by any family reasons, and their imagination being more in harmony with Christianity than with Italian Paganism, these women amused themselves with the recitals of the deed of the gods upon earth. Philostratus enchanted them with his "Life of Apollonius Tyane." Perhaps they had more than one secret affinity with Christianity. Certainly Heliogabalus was mad; and yet his chimera of a central, Monotheistic worship, established at Rome, and absorbing all the other worships, proved that the narrow circle of ideas of the Antonines was broken. Alexander Severus went still farther. He was sympathetic with the Christians: not content with according them liberty, he placed Jesus in his lararium with a touching eclecticism. Peace seemed to be made, not, as under Constantine, by the defection of one of the parties, but by a large reconciliation. The same thing was seen again under Philip the Arab, in the East under Zenobia, and generally under those emperors whose foreign origin placed them beyond Roman patriotism.

The struggle redoubled in rage when those grand reformers, Diocletian and Maximian, animated by the ancient spirit, believed themselves able to give new life for the empire by holding it to the narrow circle of Roman ideas. The Church triumphed through its martyrs. Roman pride was humbled. Constantine saw the interior strength of the Church. The population of Asia Minor, Syria, Thrace, and Macedonia, in a word the eastern part of the empire, was already more than half Christian. His mother, who had been a servant in an inn at Nicomedia, dazzled his eyes with the picture of an Eastern empire having its centre near Nicæa or Nicomedia, whose nerves should be the bishops and those multitudes of poor matriculates of the Church who controlled opinion in large cities. Constantine made the empire Christian. From the Occidental point of view, that was astonishing; for the Christians were still but a feeble minority in the West: in the Orient, the politics of Constantine was not only natural, but commanded.

Wonderful thing! The city of Rome received from that politics the heaviest blow it had ever suffered. Christianity was successful under Constantine; but it was Oriental Christianity. In building a new Rome on the Bosphorus, Constantine made the old Rome the capital of the West alone. The cataclysms which followed, the invasions of the barbarians who spared Constantinople, and fell upon Rome with all their weight, reduced the ancient capital of the world to a limited and often humble condition. That ecclesiastical primacy of Rome which burst with so much effect upon the second and third centuries flourished no longer when the Orient had an existence and a separate capital. Constantine was the real author of the schism of the Latin Church and the Church of the Orient.

Rome took its revenge, principally by the seriousness and depth of its spirit of organization. What men were St. Sylvester, St. Damasus, and Gregory the Great! With an admirable courage they labored for the conversion of the barbarians, attached them to themselves, and made them their friends and subjects. The master-work of its politics was its alliance with the Carlovingian house, and the bold stroke by which it re-established in that house the empire which had been dead three hundred years. The Church of Rome rose again more powerful than ever, and became again the centre of all the grand affairs of the Occident during eight centuries.

Here my task is ended, gentlemen. You will confide to others the care of recounting the prodigious history of the feudal church, its grandeurs and its abuses. Another still will show you the re-action against these abuses, — Protestantism returning to the primitive idea of Christianity, and dividing, in its turn, the Latin Church. Each one of these grand historical pages will have its charm and its instruction. What I have recounted to you is full of grandeur. One is impartial only to the dead. Since Catholicism was an inimical power, a danger to the liberty of the human mind, it was right to oppose it. Our age is the age of history, because it is the age of doubt upon dogmatic matters: it is the age in which, without entering into the discussion of systems, an enlightened mind says to itself, "If, since right exists, and so many thousand symbols have made the pretension of presenting the complete truth, and if this pretension is always found vain, is it indeed probable that I shall be more happy than so many others, and that the truth has awaited my coming here below in order to make its definite revelation?" There is no definite revelation. It is the touching effort of man to render his destiny supportable. But its reward is not disdain, it is gratitude. Whoever believes that he has something to teach us concerning our destiny and our end should be welcome. Recall the account in your old histories of the judicious and discreet words of the Saxon chief of Northumbria, in the assembly where the question was discussed concerning the adoption of the doctrine of the Roman missionaries.

"Perhaps thou rememberest, O king! something which happens sometimes in the winter days, when thou art seated at table with thy captains and thy men-at-arms; that a good fire is lighted, that thy chamber is very warm, while it rains, snows, and blows without. There comes a little bird, which crosses the chamber on the wing, entering at one door, and going out by the other. The moment of this passage is full of sweetness for him: he no more feels the rain nor the storm. The bird is gone in an instant, and from the winter he passes again into the winter. Such seems to me the life of men on this earth, and its course of a moment, compared to the length of time which precedes and follows it. The time before birth and after death is gloomy. It torments us by its impossibility of comprehension: if, then, the new doctrine can teach us any thing a little certain, it deserves to be considered."

Alas! the Roman missionaries did not bear this minimum of certainty, with which the old

Northumbrian chief, sage as he was, declared himself content. Life always appears to us a short passage between two long nights. Happy those who can sleep in the empty noise of menaces which trouble at times the human conscience, and should no more than cradle it! One thing is certain: it is the paternal smile which at certain hours pierces nature, attesting that one eye regards us, and one heart follows us. Let us guard ourselves from all absolute formula which might become one day an obstacle to the free expansion of our spirits. There is no religious communion which does not still possess some gifts of life and pardon; but it is on the condition only that an humble docility succeeds sympathetic adhesion. The comparison of the regiment, invented by Clement Romanus, and since so many times repeated, ought to be utterly abandoned.

You wished that I should recall to you the grandeurs of Catholicism in its finest epoch. I thank you for it. Some associations of childhood, the most profound of all, attach me to Catholicism; and, although I am separated from it, I am often tempted to say, as Job said (at least in our Latin version), "*Etiam si occideret me, in ipso sperabo.*" This great Catholic family is too numerous not to have still a grand future. The strange excesses which it has supported during fifty years, this unequalled pontificate of Pius IX., the most astonishing in history, cannot be terminated in any ordinary way. There will be thunders and lightnings such as accompany all the great judgment-days of God. And will she have much to do in order to still remain acceptable to those who love her, — this old mother, who will not die so soon? Perhaps she will find, in order to arrest the arms of her conqueror, which is modern reason, some magician's arts, some words such as Balder murmured.

The Catholic Church is a woman: let us distrust the charming words of her agony. Let us imagine that she says to us, "My children, every thing here below is but a symbol and a dream. In this world there is only one little ray of light which pierces the darkness, and seems to be the reflection of a benevolent will. Come into my bosom, where one finds forgetfulness. For those who wish fetishes, I have them; to those who wish works, I offer them; for those who wish intoxication of heart, I have the milk of my breast, which will make drunk; for those who desire love, I have an abundance; to those who crave irony, I pour out freely. Come all: the time of dogmatic sadness is past. I have music and incense for your funerals, flowers for your marriages, the joyous welcome of bells for your new-born ones." Ah, well! if she should say that, our embarrassment would be extreme. But she never will.

Your great and glorious England has resolved, gentlemen, the practical part of the question. It is as easy to trace the line of conduct which the state and individuals should follow in the same matter, as it is impossible to arrive at a theoretic solution of the religious problem. All this may be conveyed in a single word, gentlemen, — *liberty*. What could be more simple? Faith does not control itself. We believe what we believe true. No one is bound to believe what he thinks false, whether it is false or not. To deny liberty of thought is a sort of contradiction. From liberty of thought to the right to express one's thought, there is but one step; for right is the same for all. I have no right to prevent a person from expressing his mind; but no one has the right to prevent me from expressing mine. Here is a theory which will appear very humble to the learned doctors who believe themselves to be in possession of absolute truth. We have a great advantage over them, gentlemen. They are obliged to be persecutors in order to be consistent; to us it is permitted to be tolerant, — tolerant for all, even for those, who, if they could, would not be so to us. Yes, let us even make this paradox: liberty is the best weapon against the enemies of liberty. Some fanatics say to us with sincerity, "We take your liberty, because you owe it to us according to your principles; but you shall not have ours, because we do not owe it to you." Ah, well! let us give them liberty all the same, and we do not imagine that in this exchange we shall be duped. No: liberty is the great dissolvent of all fanaticisms. In giving back liberty to my enemy, who would suppress me if he had the power, I shall really make him the worst gift. I oblige him to drink a strong beverage which shall turn his head, while I shall keep my own. Science supports the strange *régime* of liberty: fanaticism and superstition do not support it. We do more harm to dogmatism by treating it with an implacable sweetness than by persecuting it. By this sweetness we even inculcate the principle which destroys all dogmatism at its root, by understanding that all metaphysical controversy is sterile, and that, for this reason, the truth for each one is as he believes it. The essential, then, is not to silence dangerous teaching, and hush the discordant voice: the essential is to place the human mind in a state in which the mass can see the uselessness of its rage. When this spirit becomes the atmosphere of society, the fanatic can no longer live. He is conquered by a pervading gentleness. If, instead of conducting Polyeuctus to punishment, the Roman magistrate had dismissed him smiling, and taken him amicably by the hand, Polyeuctus would not have continued: perhaps even in his old age he would have laughed at his escapade, and would have become a man of good sense.

CONFERENCE,

ROYAL ACADEMY, LONDON, APRIL 16, 1880.

MARCUS AURELIUS.

CONFERENCE AT THE ROYAL INSTITUTION.

MARCUS AURELIUS.

LADIES AND GENTLEMEN, — I have accepted with great pleasure the invitation to address you in this illustrious institution devoted to the noblest researches of science and of true philosophy. I have dreamed since my childhood of this island, where I have so many friends, and which I visit so tardily.

I am a Briton of France. In our old books, England is always called the Island of the Saints; and, in truth, all our saints of Armorican Brittany, those saints of doubtful orthodoxy, who, if they were again alive, would be more in harmony with us than with the Jesuits, came from the Island of Britain. I have seen in their chapel the trough of stone in which they crossed the sea. Of all races, the Britain race is that which has ever taken religion the most seriously. Even when the progress of reflection has shown us that some articles among the catalogues of things which we have always regarded as fixed should be modified, we never break away from the symbol under which we have from the first approved the ideal.

For our faith is not contained in obscure metaphysical propositions: it is in the affirmations of the heart. I have therefore chosen for my discourse to you, not one of those subtleties which divide, but one of those themes, dear to the soul, which bring nearer, and reconcile. I shall speak to you of that book resplendent with the divine spirit, that manual of submissive life which the most godly of men has left us, — the Cæsar, Marcus Aurelius Antonine. It is the glory of sovereigns that the most irreproachable model of virtue may be found in their ranks, and that the most beautiful lessons of patience and of self-control may come from a condition which one naturally believes to be subject to all the seductions of pleasure and of vanity.

I.

The inheritance of wisdom with a throne is always rare: I find in history but two striking examples of it, — in India, the succession of the three Mongol emperors, Bâber, Hoomâyoon, and Akbar; at Rome, at the head of the greatest empire that ever existed, the two admirable reigns of Antonine the Pious and Marcus Aurelius. Of the last two, I consider Antonine the greatest. His goodness did not lead him into faults: he was not tormented with that internal trouble which disturbed without ceasing the heart of his adopted son. This strange malady, this restless study of himself, this demon of scrupulousness, this fever of perfection, are signs of a less strong and distinguished nature. As the finest thoughts are those which are not written, Antonine had in this respect also a superiority over Marcus Aurelius. But let us add that we should be ignorant of Antonine, if Marcus Aurelius had not transmitted to us that exquisite portrait of his adopted father, in which he seems to have applied himself, through humility, to painting the picture of a better man than himself.

It is he who has sketched in the first book of his "Thoughts," — that admirable background where the noble and pure forms of his father, mother, grandfather, and tutors, move in a celestial light. Thanks to Marcus Aurelius, we are able to understand how these old Roman families, who had seen the reign of the wicked emperors, still retained honesty, dignity, justice, the civil, and, if I may dare to say it, the republican spirit. They lived there in admiration of Cato, of Brutus, of Thrasea, and of the great stoics whose souls had never bowed under tyranny. The reign of Domitian was abhorred by them. The sages who had endured it without submission were honored as heroes. The accession of the

Antonines was only the coming to power of the society of sages, of whose just anger Tacitus has informed us, — a society of wise men formed by the league of all those who had revolted against the despotism of the first Cæsars.

The salutary principle of adoption made the imperial court of the second century a true cradle of virtue. The noble and learned Nerva, in establishing this principle, assured the happiness of the human race during almost a hundred years, and gave to the world the best century of progress of which any knowledge has been preserved. The sovereignty thus possessed in common by a group of choice men who delegated it or shared it, according to the needs of the moment, lost a part of that attraction which renders it so dangerous.

Men came to the throne without seeking it, but also without the right of birth, or in any sense the divine right: men came there understanding themselves, experienced, having been long prepared. The empire was a civil burden which each accepted in his turn, without dreaming of hastening the hour. Marcus Aurelius was made emperor so young, that the idea of ruling had scarcely occurred to him, and had not for a moment exercised its charm upon his mind.

At eight years, when he was already *præsul* of the Salian priests, Hadrian remarked this sad child, and loved him for his good-nature, his docility, and his incapability of falsehood. At eighteen years the empire was assured to him. He awaited it patiently for twenty-two years. The evening when Antonine, feeling himself about to die, after having given to the tribune the watchword, *Æquanimitas*, commanded the golden statue of Fortune, which was always in the apartment of the emperor, to be borne into that of his adopted son, he experienced neither surprise nor joy.

He had long been sated with all joys, without having tasted them: he had seen the absolute vanity of them by the profoundness of his philosophy.

The great inconvenience of practical life, and that which renders it insupportable to a superior man, is, that, if one carries into it the principles of the ideal, talents become defects; so that very often the accomplished man is less successful in it than one who is fitted by egotism or ordinary routine. Three or four times the virtue of Marcus Aurelius came near being his ruin. The first fault into which it led him was that of sharing the empire with Lucius Verus, to whom he was under no obligation. Verus was a frivolous and worthless man. Prodigies of goodness and delicacy were necessary in order to prevent his committing disastrous follies. The wise emperor, earnest and industrious, took with him in his *lectica* (sedan) the senseless colleague whom he had given himself. He persisted in treating him seriously: he never once revolted against this sorry companionship. Like all well-bred men, Marcus Aurelius discommoded himself continually: his manners came from a general habit of firmness and dignity. Souls of this kind, either from respect for human nature, or in order not to wound others, resign themselves to the appearance of seeing no evil. Their life is a perpetual dissimulation.

According to some, he even deceived himself, since, in his intimate intercourse with the gods, on the borders of the Granicus, speaking of his unworthy wife, he thanked them for having given him a wife "so amiable, so affectionate, so pure." I have shown elsewhere that the patience, or, if one chooses, the weakness, on this point, of Marcus Aurelius, has been somewhat exaggerated. Faustina had faults: the greatest one was that she disliked the friends of her husband; and, as these friends wrote history, she has paid the penalty before posterity. But a discriminating critic has no trouble in showing the exaggerations of the legend. Every thing indicates that Faustina at first found happiness and love in that villa at Lorium, or in that beautiful retreat at Lanuvium upon the highest points of the Alban mount, which Marcus Aurelius described to his tutor

Fronto as an abode full of the purest joys. Then she became weary of too much wisdom. Let us tell all: the beautiful sentences of Marcus Aurelius, his austere virtue, his perpetual melancholy, might have become tiresome to a young and capricious woman possessed of an ardent temperament and marvellous beauty. He understood it, suffered it, and spoke not. Faustina remained always his "very good and very faithful wife." No one succeeded, even after her death, in persuading him to give up this pious lie. In a bas-relief which is still seen in the Museum of the Capitol at Rome, while Faustina is borne to heaven by a messenger of the gods, the excellent emperor regards her with a look full of love. It seems that at last he had deceived himself, and forgotten all. But through what a struggle he must have passed in order to do this! During long years, a sickness at heart slowly consumed him. The desperate effort which was the essence of his philosophy, this frenzy of renunciation, carried sometimes even to sophism, concealed an immense wound at the bottom. How necessary it must have been to bid adieu to happiness in order to reach such an excess! No one will ever understand all that this poor wounded heart suffered, the bitterness which that pale face concealed, always calm, always smiling. It is true that the farewell to happiness is the beginning of wisdom and the surest means of finding peace. There is nothing so sweet as the return of joy which follows the renunciation of joy; nothing so keen, so profound, so charming, as the enchantment of the disenchanted.

Some historians, more or less imbued with that policy which believes itself to be superior, because it is not suspected of any philosophy, have naturally sought to prove that so accomplished a man was a bad administrator and a mediocre sovereign. It appears, in fact, that Marcus Aurelius sinned more than once by too much lenity. But never was there a reign more fruitful in reforms and progress. The public charity founded by Nerva and Trajan was admirably developed by him. New schools were established for poor children; the superintendents of provisions became functionaries of the first rank, and were chosen with extreme care; while the wants of poor young girls were cared for by the Institute of *Jeunes Faustiniennes*. The principle that the state has duties in some degree paternal towards its members (a principle which should be remembered with gratitude, even when it has been dispensed with),—this principle, I say, was proclaimed for the first time in the world by Trajan and his successors. Neither the puerile pomp of Oriental kingdoms, founded on the baseness and stupidity of men, nor the pedantic pride of the kingdoms of the middle ages, founded on an exaggerated sentiment for hereditary succession, and on a simple faith in the rights of blood, could give an idea of the utterly republican sovereignty of Nerva, Trajan, Hadrian, Antonine, and Marcus Aurelius.

Nothing of the prince by hereditary or divine right, nothing of the military chieftain: it was a sort of grand civil magistracy, without resembling a court in any way, or depriving the emperor of his private character. Marcus Aurelius, in particular, was neither much nor little a king in the true sense of the word. His fortune was immense, but all employed for good: his aversion for "the Cæsars," whom he considered as a species of Sardanapali, magnificent, debauched, and cruel, burst out at each instant. The civility of his manners was extreme. He gave to the Senate all its ancient importance: when he was at Rome, he never missed a session, and left his place only when the Consul had pronounced the formula, "*Nihil vos moramar, patres conscripti.*" Almost every year of his reign he made war, and he made it well, although he found in it only *ennui*. His listless campaigns against the Quadi and Marcomanni were very well conducted: the disgust which he felt for them did not prevent his most conscientious attention to them. It was in the course of one of these expeditions, that, encamped on the banks of the Granicus, in the midst of the monotonous plains of Hungary, he wrote the most beautiful pages of the exquisite book which has revealed his whole soul to us. It is probable, that, when very young, he kept a journal of his secret thoughts. He inscribed there the maxims to which he had recourse in order to fortify himself, the reminiscences of his favorite authors, the passages of the moralists which appealed most to him, the principles which had sustained him through the day, sometimes the reproaches which his scrupulous conscience addressed to him. "One seeks for himself solitary retreats, rustic cottages, seashore, or mountains: like others, thou lovest to dream of these good things. To what end, since it is permitted to thee to retire within thy soul each hour? Man has nowhere a more tranquil retreat, above all, if he has within himself those things, the contemplation of which will calm him. Learn, then, how to enjoy this retreat, and there renew thy strength. Let there be there those short fundamental maxims, which above all will give again serenity to thy soul, and restore thee to a state in which to support with resignation the world to which thou shouldest return."

During the sad winters of the North, this consolation became still more necessary to him. He was nearly sixty years old: old age was premature with him. One evening all the pictures of his pious youth returned to his remembrance, and he passed some delicious hours in calculating how much he owed to each one of the virtuous beings who had surrounded him.

"Examples of my grandfather Verus, — sweetness of manners, unchangeable patience."

"Qualities which one valued in my father, the souvenir which he has left me, — modesty, manly character."

"To imitate the piety of my mother, her benevolence; to abstain, like her, not only from doing evil, but from conceiving the thought of it; to lead her frugal life, which so little resembled the habitual luxury of the rich."

Then appeared to him, in turn, Diagnotus, who had inspired him with a taste for philosophy, and made agreeable to his eyes the pallet, the covering made of a simple skin, and all the apparel of Hellenic discipline; Junius Rusticus, who taught him to avoid all affectation of elegance in style, and loaned him the Conversations of Epictetus; Apollonius of Chalcis, who realized the Stoic ideal of extreme firmness and perfect sweetness; Sextus of Chaeroncia, so grave and so good; Alexander the grammarian, who censured with such refined politeness; Fronto, "who taught him the envy, duplicity, and hypocrisy of a tyrant, and the hardness which may exist in the heart of a patrician;" his brother Severus, "who made him understand Thrasia, Helvidius, Cato, Brutus, who gave him the idea of what a free government is, where the rule is the natural equality of the citizens and the equality of their rights; of a royalty which places before all else the respect for the liberty of the ctizens;" and, rising above all others in his immaculate grandeur, Antonine, his father by adoption, whose picture he traces for us with redoubled gratitude and love. "I thank the gods," said he finally, "for having given me good ancestors, good parents, a good sister, good teachers, and in my surroundings, in my relations, in my friends, men almost all filled with goodness. I never allowed myself to be wanting in deference towards them: from my natural disposition, I could sometimes have shown irreverence; but the benevolence of the gods never permitted the occasion to present itself. I am also indebted to the gods, who preserved pure the flower of my youth, for having been reared under the rule of a prince, and a father who strove to free my soul from all trace of pride, to make me understand that it is possible, while living in a palace, to dispense with guards, with splendid clothes, with torches, with statues, to teach me, in short, that a prince can almost contract his life within the limits of that of a simple citizen, without, on that account, showing less nobility and vigor when he comes to be an emperor, and transact the affairs of state. They gave me a brother, whose manners were a continual exhortation to watch over myself, while his deference and attachment should have made the joy of my heart.

"Thanks to the gods again, that I have made haste to raise those who have cared for my education, to the honors which they seemed to desire. They have enabled me to understand Apollonius, Rusticus, Maximus, and have held out to me, surrounded with brilliant light, the picture of a life conformed to nature. I have fallen short of it in the end, it is true; but it is my fault. If my body has long supported the rude life which I lead; if, in spite of my frequent neglect of Rusticus, I have never overstepped the bounds, or done any thing of which I should repent; if my mother, who died young, was able, nevertheless, to pass her last years near me; if, whenever I have wished to succor the poor or afflicted, money has never been wanting; if I have never needed to accept any thing from others; if I have a wife of an amiable, affectionate, and pure character; if I have found many capable men for the education of my children; if, at the beginning of my passion for philosophy, I did not become the prey of a sophist, — it is to the gods that I owe it all. Yes, so many blessings could only be the result of the aid of the gods and a happy fortune."

This divine candor breathes in every page. No one has ever written more simply than did he for the sole purpose of unburdening his heart to God, his only witness. There is not a shadow of system in it. Marcus Aurelius, to speak exactly, had no philosophy: although he owed almost every thing to stoicism transformed by the Roman spirit, it is of no school. According to our idea, he has too little curiosity; for he knows not all that a contemporary of Ptolemy and Galen should know: he has some opinions on the system of the world, which were not up to the highest science of his time. But his moral thought, thus detached from all alliance with a system, reaches a singular height. The author of the book, "The Imitation," himself, although free from the quarrels of the schools, does not rise to this, for his manner of feeling is essentially Christian. Take away his Christian dogmas, and his book retains only a portion of its charm. The book of Marcus Aurelius, having no dogmatic base, preserves its freshness eternally. Every one, from the atheist, or he who believes himself one, to the man who is the most devoted to the especial creeds of each worship, can find in it some fruits of edification. It is the most purely human book which exists. It deals with no question of controversy. In theology, Marcus Aurelius floats between pure Deism, Polytheism interpreted in a physical sense according to the manner of the Stoics, and a sort of cosmic Pantheism. He holds not much more firmly to one hypothesis than to the other, and he uses indiscriminately the three vocabularies of the Deist, Polytheist, and Pantheist. His considerations have always two sides, according as God and the soul have, or have not, reality. It is the reasoning which we do each hour; for, if the most complete Materialism is right, we who have believed in truth and goodness shall be no more duped than others. If Idealism is right, we have been the true sages, and we have been wise in the only manner which becomes us, that is to say, with no selfish waiting, without having looked for a remuneration.

II.

We here touch a great secret of moral philosophy and religion. Marcus Aurelius has no speculative philosophy; his theology is utterly contradictory; he has no idea founded upon the soul and immortality. How could he be so moral without the beliefs that are now regarded as the foundations of morality? how so profoundly religious, without having professed one of the dogmas of what is called natural religion? It is important to make this inquiry.

The doubts, which, to the view of speculative reason, hover above the truths of natural religion, are not, as Kant has admirably shown, accidental doubts, capable of being removed, belonging, as is sometimes imagined, to certain conditions of the human mind. These doubts are inherent to the nature even of these truths, if one may say it without a paradox; and, if these doubts were removed, the truths with which they quarrel would disappear at the same time. Let us suppose, in short, a direct, positive proof, evident to all, of future sufferings and rewards: where will be the merit of doing good? They would be but fools whom gayety of heart should hasten to damnation. A crowd of base souls would secure their salvation without concealment: they would, in a sense, force the divine power. Who does not see, that, in such a system, there is neither morality nor religion? In the moral and religious order it is indispensable to believe without demonstration. It deals not with certainty: it acts by faith. This is what Deism forgets, with its habits of intemperate affirmation. It forgets that creeds too precise concerning human destiny would destroy all moral merit. For us, they would say that we should do as did St. Louis when he was told of the miraculous wafer, — we should refuse to see it. What need have we of these brutal proofs which trammel our liberty?

We should fear to become assimilated to those speculators in virtue, or those vulgar cowards, who mingle with spiritual things the gross selfishness of practical life. In the days which followed the belief in the resurrection of Jesus, this sentiment was manifested in the most touching manner. The faithful in heart, the sensitive ones, preferred to believe without seeing. "Blessed are they that have not seen, and yet have believed," became the word for the time. Charming words! Eternal symbol of tender and generous Idealism, which has a horror of touching with the hands that which should only be seen with the heart!

Our good Marcus Aurelius, on this point as on all others, was in advance of the ages. He never cared to argue with himself concerning God and the soul. As if he had read the "Criticism of Practical Reason," he saw clearly, that, where the Infinite is concerned, no formula is absolute; and that, in such matters, one has no chance of seeing the truth during his life, without much self-contradiction. He distinctly separates moral beauty from all theoretical theology. He allows duty to depend on no metaphysical opinion of the First Cause. The intimate union with an unseen god was never carried to a more unheard-of delicacy. "To offer to the government of God that which is within thee, — a strong being ripened by age, a friend of the public good, a Roman, an emperor, a soldier at his post awaiting the signal of the trumpet, a man ready to quit life without regret." "There are many grains of incense destined to the same altar: one falls sooner, the other later, in the fire; but the difference is nothing." "Man should live according to nature during the few days that are given him on the earth, and, when the moment of leaving it comes, should submit himself sweetly, as an olive, which, in falling, blesses the tree which has produced it, and renders thanks to the branch which has borne it." "All that which thou arrangest is suited to me, O Cosmos! Nothing of that which comes from thee is premature or backward to me. I find my fruit in that which thy seasons bear, O Nature! From thee comes all; in thee is all; to thee all returns." "O man! thou hast been a citizen in the great city: what matters it to thee to have remained three or five years? That which is governed by laws is unjust for no one. What is there, then, so sorrowful in being sent from the city, not by a tyrant, not by an unjust judge, but by the same nature which allowed thee to enter there? It is as if a comedian is discharged from the theatre by the same prætor who engaged him. But wilt thou say, 'I have not played the five acts; I have played but three?' Thou sayest well; but in life three acts suffice to complete the entire piece. . . . Go, then, content, since he who dismisses thee is content."

Is this to say that he never revolted against the strange fate which leaves man alone face to face with the needs of devotion, of sacrifice, of heroism, and nature with its transcendent immorality, its supreme disdain for virtue? No. Once at least the absurdity, the colossal iniquity, of death, strikes him. But soon his temperament, completely mortified, resumes its power, and he becomes calm. "How happens it that the gods, who have ordered all things so well, and with so much love for men, should have forgotten one thing only; that is, that men of tried virtue, who during their lives have had a sort of interchange of relations with divinity, who have made themselves loved by it on account of their pious acts and their sacrifices, live not after death, but may be extinguished forever?

"Since it is so, be sure, that, if it should be otherwise, they (the gods) would not have failed; for, if it had been just, it would have been possible; if it had been suitable to nature, nature would have permitted it. Consequently, when it is not thus, strengthen thyself in this consideration, that it was not necessary that it should be thus. Thou thyself seest plainly that to make such a demand is to dispute his right with God. Now, we would not thus contend with the gods if they were not absolutely good and absolutely just: if they are so, they have allowed nothing to make a part of the order of the world which is contrary to justice and right."

Ah! is it too much resignation, ladies and gentlemen? If it is veritably thus, we have the right to complain. To say, that, if this world has not its counterpart, the man who is sacrificed to truth or right ought to leave it content, and absolve the gods, — that is too *naïve*. No, he has a right to blaspheme them. For, in short, why has his credulity been thus abused? Why should he have been endowed with deceitful instincts, of which he has been the honest dupe? Wherefore is this premium given to the frivolous or wicked man? Is it, then, he who is not deceived who is the wise man? Then cursed be the gods who so adjudge their preferences! I desire that the future may be an enigma; but, if there is no future, then this world is a frightful ambuscade. Take notice that our wish is not that of the vulgar clown. We wish not to see the chastisement of the culpable, nor to meddle with the interests of our virtue. Our wish has no selfishness: it is simply to be, to remain in accord with light, to continue the thought we have begun, to know more of it, to enjoy some day that truth which we seek with so much labor, to see the triumph of the good which we have loved. Nothing is more legitimate. The worthy emperor, moreover, was also sensible of it: "What! the light of a lamp burns until the moment in which it is extinguished, and loses nothing of its brilliancy, and the truth, justice, temperance, which are in thee shall be extinguished with thee!" All his life was passed in this noble hesitation. If he sinned, it was through too much piety. Less resigned, he would have been more just; for surely to demand that there should be an intimate and sympathetic witness of the struggles which we endure for goodness and truth is not to ask too much.

It is possible, also, that if his philosophy had been less exclusively moral, if it had implied a more curious study of history and of the universe, it would have escaped a certain excessive rigor. Like the ascetic Christians, Marcus Aurelius sometimes carried renunciation to dryness and subtlety. One feels that this calmness, which never belies itself, is obtained through an immense effort. Certainly, evil had never an attraction for him: he had no passion to struggle against. "Whatever one may do or say," writes he, "it is necessary that I should be a good man; as the emerald might say, 'Whatever one may say or do, I must remain an emerald, and retain my color.'" But, in order to hold one's self always upon the icy summit of stoicism, it is necessary to do cruel violence to nature, and to cut away from it more than one noble element. This perpetual repetition of the same reasoning, the thousand figures under which he seeks to represent to himself the vanity of all things, these frequently artless proofs of universal frivolity, testify to strifes which he has passed through in order to extinguish all desire in himself. At times we find in it something harsh and sad. The reading of Marcus Aurelius strengthens, but it does not console: it leaves a void in the soul which is at once cruel and delightful, which one would not exchange for full satisfaction. Humility, renunciation, severity towards self, were never carried further. Glory — that last illusion of great souls — is reduced to nothingness. It is needful to do right without disturbing one's self as to whether any one knows that we do it. He perceives that history will speak of him: he sometimes dreams of the men of the past with whom the future will associate him. "If they have only played the part of tragic actors," said he, "no one has condemned me to imitate them." The absolute mortification at which he had arrived had destroyed the last fibre of self-love in him.

The consequences of this austere philosophy might have been hardness and obstinacy. It is here that the rare goodness of the nature of Marcus Aurelius shines out in its full brilliancy. His severity is only for himself. The fruit of this great tension of soul is an infinite benevolence. All his life was a study of how to return good for evil. At evening, after some sad experience of human perversity, he wrote only as follows: "If thou canst, correct them; on the other hand, remember that thou shouldest exercise benevolence towards those who have been given to thee. The gods themselves are benevolent to men: they aid them, — so great is their goodness! — to acquire health, riches, glory. Thou art permitted to be like the gods." Another day, some one was very wicked; for see what he wrote upon his tablets: "Such is the order of nature: men of this sort must act thus from necessity. To wish it to be otherwise is to wish that the fig-tree shall bear no figs. Remember, thou, in one word, this thing: in a very short time thou and he will die; soon after, your names even will be known no more." The thoughts of a universal pardon recur without ceasing. At times a scarcely perceptible smile is mingled with this charming goodness, — "The best method of avenging one's self upon the wicked is not to be like them;" or a light stroke of pride, — "It is a royal thing to hear evil said of one's self when one does right." One day he thus reproached himself: "Thou hast forgotten," said he, "what holy relationship unites each man to the human race, — a relationship not of blood, or of birth, but the participation in the same intelligence. Thou hast forgotten that the reasoning power of each one is a god, derived from the Supreme Being."

In the business of life he was always exact, although a little ingenuous, as very good men usually are. The nine reasons for forbearance which he valued for himself (book xi. art. 18) show us his charming good-nature before family troubles, which perhaps came to him through his unworthy son. "If, upon occasion," said he to himself, "thou exhortest him quietly, and shalt give to him without anger some lessons like these, — 'No, my child; we are born for each other. It is not I who suffer the evil, it is thou who doest it thyself, my child!' — show him adroitly, by a general consideration, that such is the rule; that neither the bees, nor the animals who live naturally in herds, resemble him. Say this without mockery or insult, with an air of true affection, with a heart which is not excited by anger; not as a pedant, not for the sake of being admired by those who are present; think only of him."

Commodus (if it was for him that he thus acted) was, without doubt, little touched by this good paternal rhetoric. One of the maxims of the excellent emperor was, that the wicked are unhappy, that one is only wicked in spite of himself, and through ignorance. He pitied those who were not like himself: he did not believe that he had the right to obtrude himself upon them.

He well understood the baseness of men; but he did not avow it. This willing blindness is the defect of choice spirits. The world not being all that they could wish, they lie to themselves in order not to see it as it is. From thence arises an expediency in their judgments. In Marcus Aurelius, this expediency sometimes provokes us a little. If we wished to believe him, his instructors, several of whom were men of mediocrity, were, without exception, superior men. One would say that every one near him had been virtuous. This is carried to such a point, that one is forced to ask if the brother for whom he pronounces such a grand eulogy in his thanks to the gods was not his adopted brother, Lucius Verus. It is certain that the good emperor was capable of strong illusions when he undertook to lend to others his own virtues.

This quality, expressed as an ancient opinion, especially by the pen of the Emperor Julian, caused him to commit an enormous error, which was that of not disinheriting Commodus. This is one of those things which it is easy to say at a distance, when there are no obstacles present, and when one reasons without facts. It is forgotten at first that the emperors, who, after Nerva, made adoption so fruitful a political system, had no sons. Adoption, with the exheredation of the son or grandson, occurred in the first century of the empire without good results. Marcus Aurelius was evidently from principle in favor of direct inheritance, in which he saw the advantage of the prevention of competition.

After the birth of Commodus, in 161, he presented him alone to the people, although he had a twin-brother: he frequently took him in his arms and renewed this act, which was a sort of proclamation. In 166 Lucius Verus demanded that the two sons of Marcus, Commodus and Annius Verus, should be made Cæsars. In 172 Commodus shared with his father the title of Germanicus. In 173, after the repression of the revolt of Avidius, the Senate, in order to recognize in some way the family disinterestedness which Marcus Aurelius had shown, demanded by acclamation the empire and the tribunitial power for Commodus.

Already the natural wickedness of the latter had betrayed itself by more than one symptom known to his tutors; but how shall one foresee the future from a few naughty acts of a child of twelve years? In 176-177 his father made him *Imperator*, Consul, Augustus. This was certainly an imprudence; but he was bound by his previous acts: Commodus, moreover, still restrained himself. In later years, the evil completely revealed itself. On each page of the last books of the "Thoughts," we see the trace of the martyr within the excellent father, of the accomplished emperor, who saw a monster growing up beside him, ready to succeed him, and to take in every thing through antipathy, the opposite course from that which he had believed to be for the good of men. The thought of disinheriting Commodus must, without doubt, have come often to Marcus Aurelius. But it was too late. After having associated him in the empire, after having so many times proclaimed him to the legions as perfect and accomplished, to come before the world and declare him to be unworthy would be a scandal. Marcus was caught in his own phrases, by that style of benevolent expediency which was too habitual with him. And, after all, Commodus was only seventeen years old: who could be sure that he would not reform? Even after the death of Marcus Aurelius this was hoped for. Commodus at first showed the intention of following the counsels of meritorious persons with whom his father had surrounded him.

The reproach which is made, then, against Marcus Aurelius, is not that of not having, but of having, a son. It was not his fault if the age could not support so much wisdom. In philosophy, the great emperor had placed the ideal of virtue so high, that no one would care to follow him. In politics, his benevolent optimism had enfeebled the state services, above all, the army. In religion, in order not to be too much bound by a religion of the state, of which he saw the weakness, he prepared the great triumph of the non-official worship, and left a reproach to hover above his memory, — unjust, it is true; but even its shadow should not be found in so pure a life. We touch here upon one of the most delicate points in the biography of Marcus Aurelius. It is unhappily certain, that, under his reign, Christians were condemned to death, and executed. The policy of his predecessors had been firm in this particular. Trajan, Antonine, Hadrian himself, saw in the Christians a secret sect, anti-social, dreaming of overturning the empire. Like all men true to the old Roman principles, they believed in the necessity of repressing them. There was no need of special edicts: the laws against the *cœtus illiciti*, the *illicita collegia*, were numerous. The Christians fell in the most explicit sense under the force of these laws. Truly, it would have been worthy of the wise emperor who introduced so many reforms full of humanity, to suppress the edicts which entailed such cruel and unjust consequences. But it is necessary to observe primarily, that the true spirit of liberty, as we understand it, was not then understood by any one; and that Christianity, when it was master, practised it no more than the Pagan emperors. In the second place, the abrogation of the laws against illicit societies would have been the ruin of the empire, founded essentially upon the principle that the state ought not to admit within its bosom any society differing from it. The principle was bad, according to our ideas: it is very certain, at least, that it was the corner-stone in the Roman constitution. Marcus Aurelius, far from exaggerating it, extenuated it with all his powers; and one of the glories of his reign is the extension of the right of association. However, he did not go to the root: he did not completely abolish the laws against the *collegia illicita*, and in the provinces there resulted from them some processes infinitely to be regretted. The reproach which can be made against him is the same that might be made to the rulers of our day, who do not suppress with a stroke of the pen all the laws restrictive of the liberties of re-union, of association, and of the press.

From the distance at which we stand, we can see that Marcus Aurelius, in being more completely liberal, would have been wiser. Perhaps Christianity left free would have developed in a manner less disastrous the theocratic and absolute principle which was in it; but one cannot reproach a man with not having stirred up a radical revolution on account of a prevision of what would occur several centuries after him. Trajan, Hadrian, Antonine, Marcus Aurelius, could not know the principles of general history and political economy which have been understood only in our time, and which only our last revolutious could reveal. In any case, the mansuetude of the good emperor was in this respect shielded from all reproach. No one has the right to be more exacting in this respect than was Tertullian. "Consult your annals," said he to the Roman magistrates. "You will then see that the princes who have been severe towards us are of those who have held to the honor of having been our persecutors. On the contrary, all the princes who have respected divine and human laws include but one who persecuted the Christians. We can even name one of them who declared himself their protector,— the wise Marcus Aurelius. If he did not openly revoke the edicts against our brethren, he destroyed their power by the severe penalties which he declared against their accusers." It is necessary to remember that the Roman Empire was ten or twelve times as large as France, and that the responsibility of the emperor was very little in the judgments which were rendered in the provinces. It is necessary, moreover, to recall the fact that Christianity claimed not only the liberty of worship: all the creeds which tolerated each other were allowed much freedom in the empire. Christianity and Judaism were the exceptions to this rule on account of their intolerance and spirit of exclusion.

We have, then, good reason to mourn sincerely for Marcus Aurelius. Under him philosophy reigned. One moment, thanks to him, the world was governed by the best and greatest man of his age. Frightful decadences followed; but the little casket which contained the "Thoughts" on the banks of the Granicus was saved. From it came forth that incomparable book in which Epictetus was surpassed, that Evangel of those who believe not in the supernatural, which has not been comprehended until our day. Veritable, eternal Evangel, the book of "Thoughts," which will never grow old, because it asserts no dogma. The virtue of Marcus Aurelius, like our own, rests upon reason, upon nature. St. Louis was a very virtuous man, because he was a Christian: Marcus Aurelius was the most godly of men, not because he was a Pagan, but because he was a gifted man. He was the honor of human nature, and not of an established religion. Science may yet destroy, in appearance, God and the immortal soul; but the book of the "Thoughts" will still remain young with life and truth.

The religion of Marcus Aurelius is the absolute religion, that which results from the simple fact of a high moral conscience placed face to face with the universe. It is of no race, neither of any country. No revolution, no change, no discovery, will have power to affect it.

www.ingramcontent.com/pod-product-compliance
Lightning Source LLC
Chambersburg PA
CBHW030243170426
43202CB00009B/608